Jerome
Just One More Song!

Jerome
Just One More Song!
Local, Social & Political History in the
Repertoire of a Newfoundland-Irish Singer

Kenneth S. Goldstein and Margaret Bennett
Folklore Collection

MARGARET BENNETT

FREE AUDIO RECORDING COLLECTION

Jerome: Just One More Song!
Local, Social & Political History in the Repertoire of a
Newfoundland-Irish Singer

First published 2012 by Grace Note Publications C.I.C.
Grange of Locherlour,
Ochtertyre, PH7 4JS, Scotland
www.gracenotepublications.co.uk
books@gracenotereading.co.uk

ISBN 978-1-907676-22-2

ISBN 978-1-907676-13-0 (hbk); ISBN 978-1-907676-14-7 (e-book);

Copyright © Margaret Bennett, 2012

The right of Margaret Bennett to be identified as the proprietor of this work has been asserted by her in accordance with the Copyright, Designs and Patents Act 1988

ALL RIGHTS RESERVED

No part of this book or audio files may be reproduced in any manner whatsoever, without express written permission from the publisher, except in the case of brief quotations embodied in critical articles and reviews.

A catalogue record for this book is available from the British Library

Cover photo © Margaret Bennett

Supported by

Foundation for Canadian
Studies in the UK

Grace Notes
Scotland
Handing on Tradition

Royal Conservatoire
of Scotland

Dedicated with esteem and affection
to Jerome Downey,
'A man you don't meet every day'
whose singing brought boundless pleasure,
and
to Rosie, his 'rarest of flowers'
who shared joy in his songs
as well as his journey through life

This book is also a tribute
to Kenneth S. Goldstein (1927–1995)
Folklorist Extraordinaire
who leaves an unmatched legacy
of world-wide song collection

Clach air do chàrn...
A stone on your cairn...

ACKNOWLEDGEMENTS

My debt of gratitude connected with this book goes back to 1968, when, as a student, I went to the Codroy Valley intending to record Scottish Gaelic traditions. Thanks to Allan and Mary MacArthur, who welcomed me into their home, their family and their community, it became clear that there was a also wealth of Irish, French and English tradition to be heard at ceilidhs and house-parties all over the Valley. Before long, I met Jerome Downey and his wife Rosie, who epitomized Newfoundland hospitality – the kettle on the boil, a song or tune in the air.

I am particularly grateful to Allan and Mary's grand-daughter Karen, whose close friendship goes back to when she was a girl of fourteen, accompanying me on fieldwork trips. Over the years, she and her husband Brian have shared their home and hospitality with me, as well as with Kenny in 1980. Lest I miss someone out, I dare not list all the folk in the Valley whose kindness has surrounded me, but would simply like to say an enormous thank-you to one and all.

Since 1968 I have also been enriched by the friendship of Hilda and Murdo Murray in Mt. Pearl (near St. John's), who have generously shared their home and family as well as lively discussions. I had lost count of the times I have visited, when, in 2007 I was invited to 'Festival 500' in St. John's to give a presentation on 'Sharing the Voices'. This world-class festival (held every two years) draws together singers from all over the world, who spend a week singing, then leave inspired at the power of the human voice. I would like to thank the Festival for inviting me, as it gave me the opportunity not only to enjoy that unique experience but also to share some of the recordings from the Codroy Valley. And, most unexpectedly, Jerome's brother Joe Downey came to meet me. From that time till this, he has given me continuous encouragement, having convinced me that there was a book to be written about the man who would always oblige with 'just one more song'. My sincere thanks go to Joe and to all the family members who answered questions sent to them.

I would like to thank Rochelle Goldstein for granting permission to use the tapes co-recorded with Kenny in 1980. I am grateful also for the support of their daughter Diane, President of the American Folklore Society and Professor of Folklore and Ethnomusicology at Indiana University. As Kenny and Rochelle shared several visits with us in Scotland, from the late

Seventies to the early Nineties, may this book and CD also evoke happy memories for Rochelle.

Over the years, the staff and faculty at the Folklore Department at Memorial University have been supportive of my research and I would like to thank Patricia Fulton and Pauline Cox for making copies of the original fieldwork recordings. Friends on both sides of the Atlantic who have shared discussions been invaluable and I appreciate each one, named and unnamed.

I also wish to thank the Foundation for Canadian Studies in London for their support towards the production of this book and CD. At the Royal Conservatoire of Scotland in Glasgow I have also benefited from the friendship and collegiality of Professor Celia Duffy of the Academic Department, Professor Christopher Underwood of the Department of Opera, Gordeanna McCulloch, Anne Neilson and Calum Ross of the Scottish Music Department and Bob Whitney of the Sound Technology Department. I am indebted to Writer in Residence, Alexander (Sandy) Hutchison, poet and piper, who carefully read my manuscript. Aside from catching typos and errors, he regularly made me laugh and saved me from several 'clangers' that would have otherwise embarrassed me. Any errors that turn up now are entirely my own – my heartfelt thanks to him.

Finally, I am grateful to Gonzalo Mazzei of Grace Note Publications, dynamo of the publishing world, who has taken care of the myriad of tasks that turn a manuscript into a book: cover design, typesetting, lay-out and production of both the book and CD. For Gonzalo too, this has been a largely a labour of love.

Margaret Bennett
Royal Conservatoire of Scotland
September 2012

ABBREVIATIONS

DVD 2007 'A Man You Don't Meet Everyday: Songs from the Codroy Valley'
JAF The Journal of American Folklore
JIFMC Journal of the International Folk Music Council
JSAM Journal of the Society for American Music
KG Kenneth S. Goldstein
MB Margaret Bennett
MUNFLA Memorial University of Newfoundland Folklore Archive
RLS Regional Languages Studies... Newfoundland
ROUD Roud Folksong Index, reference number

FOREWORD

Since its foundation in 1968, Memorial University of Newfoundland Folklore Archives has amassed an unrivalled collection of folksongs of the British Isles tradition. Thanks to its founder, Professor Herbert Halpert, Folklore students were inspired to make fieldwork recordings all over the province, thus helping to capture thousands of Newfoundland voices on reel-to-reel tapes. In those days, the trainee folklorist's 'Bible' was Kenneth S. Goldstein's *Guide for Fieldworkers in Folklore*, which was based on his own fieldwork experiences in the Northeast of Scotland. As a student, I found the 'set reading' to be a gift, for, besides practical advice, it provided a link with home and friends in Scotland. Furthermore, the book is introduced by Hamish Henderson, Scotland's most renowned twentieth century folklorist, singer and poet, 'father of the Scottish folk revival' and stalwart of the University of Edinburgh's School of Scottish Studies.

When he returned to the USA in 1960 and later became Professor of Folklore at the University of Pennsylvania, Goldstein proved he was no armchair academic but one of the most dynamic fieldworkers ever. As the world of Folklore is small compared to that of other scholarly disciplines, there has always been dialogue between the finest minds and practitioners in the field. Such was the relationship between Herbert Halpert in Canada, Hamish Henderson in Scotland and Kenny Goldstein in the United States, that in the late Sixties and early Seventies – before email – students benefited from their joint friendships as well as their excellent teaching.

After nine years in Canada I returned to Scotland to find that Professor Halpert had already discussed with Henderson and Goldstein the fieldwork recordings I had made in the Codroy Valley while a graduate student (1968–1974). Out of those conversations came two important collaborations: the first in 1980 when, at the invitation of Professor Goldstein, I returned to Newfoundland to take part in Kenny's mammoth recording project that eventually amassed approximately 4,000 songs. The second began in 1984, when I was appointed lecturer at the University of Edinburgh's School of Scottish Studies, often referred to as 'Hamish Henderson's department'. As colleagues of two formidable folklorists – the first for less than a week, in the Codroy Valley, and the second in Scotland, for well over a decade – I was blessed to work with two of the most inspiring Folklorists the world has ever seen.

Kenneth S. Goldstein (1927–1995) was not only a scholar of international renown but also one of the most influential figures in the folk revival of the Fifties and Sixties. There can hardly be a singer or musician anywhere in the folk scene that did not listen to the Clancy Brothers, who were recorded by Kenny Goldstein – recognizing their 'star quality' he produced their first album. Kenny had the extraordinary ability to straddle the worlds of academia, the music business and the grassroots folk music scene. He was also involved in major festivals such as the Philadelphia Folk Festival in the USA and the Mariposa Festival in Canada.

Singers and musicians on both sides of the Atlantic have come under his influence, as he was driving force behind several groundbreaking records on the Celtic Music scene. Close to the end of his life, when I went to see Kenny and Rochelle, the visit was both poignant and memorable: he spoke with joy about his years of fieldwork. Among his Newfoundland recordings, a few names stood out for him as being outstanding – Jerome was one of them. If only we had had time to bring out a record of Jerome... If only...

Now (2012), more than thirty years after we recorded him in the Codroy Valley, Jerome is celebrated as an outstanding singer. His name and his songs will live on, not only among those who had the joy of knowing him and of hearing him sing, but also among those who listen to him for the first time. This book (with CD) has been a labour of love, with gratitude to all those who have enriched my life through songs and singing. May it be a fitting tribute to Jerome who generously shared his gift of song and love of music. As he himself was fond of saying, "If the Lord made anything any better He kept it to Himself!"

Margaret Bennett
September 2012

TABLE OF CONTENTS

ACKNOWLEDGEMENTS	vi
ABBREVIATIONS	viii
FOREWORD	ix
INTRODUCTION	1
THE DOWNEYS	5
THE SINGER AND THE SONG-MAKERS	
JEROME – THE MAN HIMSELF	13
STYLE AND REPERTOIRE	20
LEARNING A SONG	25
LOCAL SONGS, WORDSMITHS AND TUNE-FINDERS	31
Paul E. Hall	32
Micky J. MacNeil	36
Hughie O'Quinn	38
SONG-MAKERS IN TRADITION AND TRANSITION	44
FOLLOWING THE LINE OF TRADITION	47
GETTING CLOSE TO THE EDGE	50
TWINS TOWNS: CHANNEL & PORT-AUX- BASQUES	53

THE SONGS & A STORY

01-Labrador Rose	59
02-The Badger Drive	61
03-The Anti-Confederation Song	67
04-The Bachelors Lament	71
05-Paul E. Hall story	77
06-Pat Malone Forgot that He Was Dead	79
07-The Road to Dundee	83
08-John Park he had Nar' One	86
09-There's a Bridle Hanging on the Wall	89
10-Teaching McFadden to Waltz	90
11-Five Boss Highway	94
12-Employment Song	100
13-I am a Roving Peddler	103
14-Galway Shawl	108
15-Mary Kate White	111
16-Paddy Haggerty's Old Leather Breeches	116
17-Come All Ye Jolly Hunters	120
18-The Cameron Men	123
19 & 20-On the Wings of a Dove	127
21-The Sealers' Song	129
22-Winnie MacNeil	136
23-The Thomas Cat	140
24-Micky Jim MacNeil	143
25-Today	148
26-Wee Cooper o' Fife	150

AFTERWORD	153
POSTSCRIPT	155
REFERENCES	157
INDEX OF TITLES AND FIRST LINES	164
FOR A FREE AUDIO RECORDING COLLECTION	171

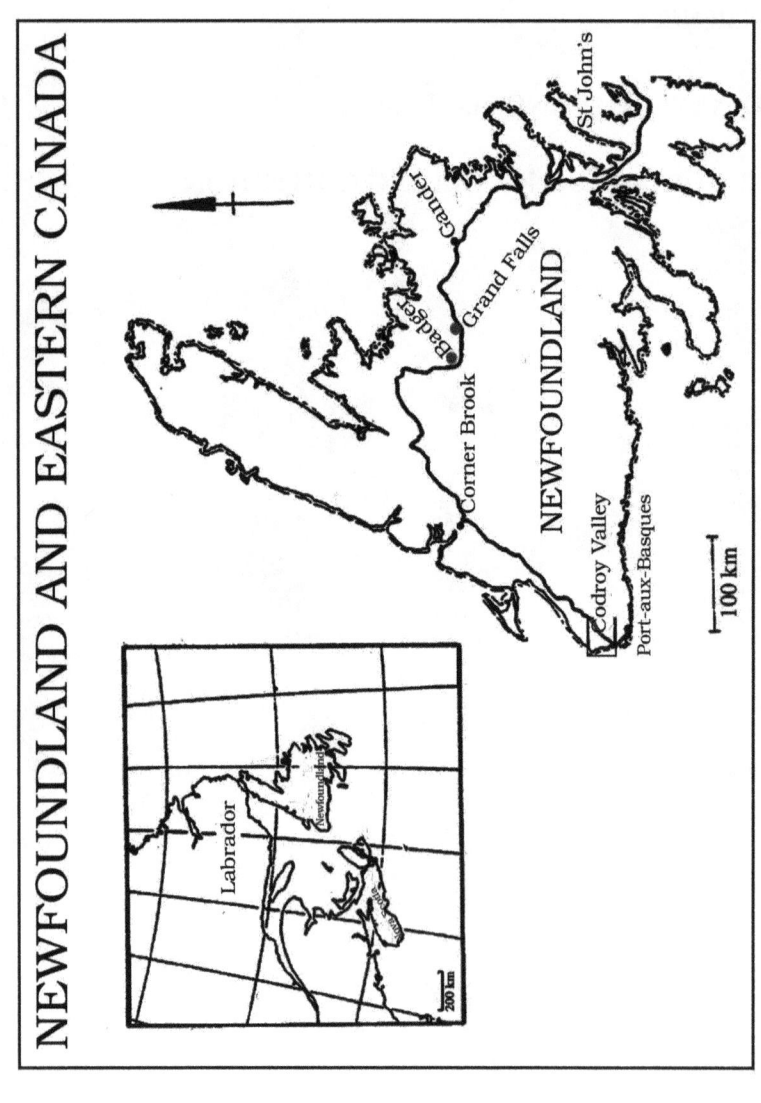

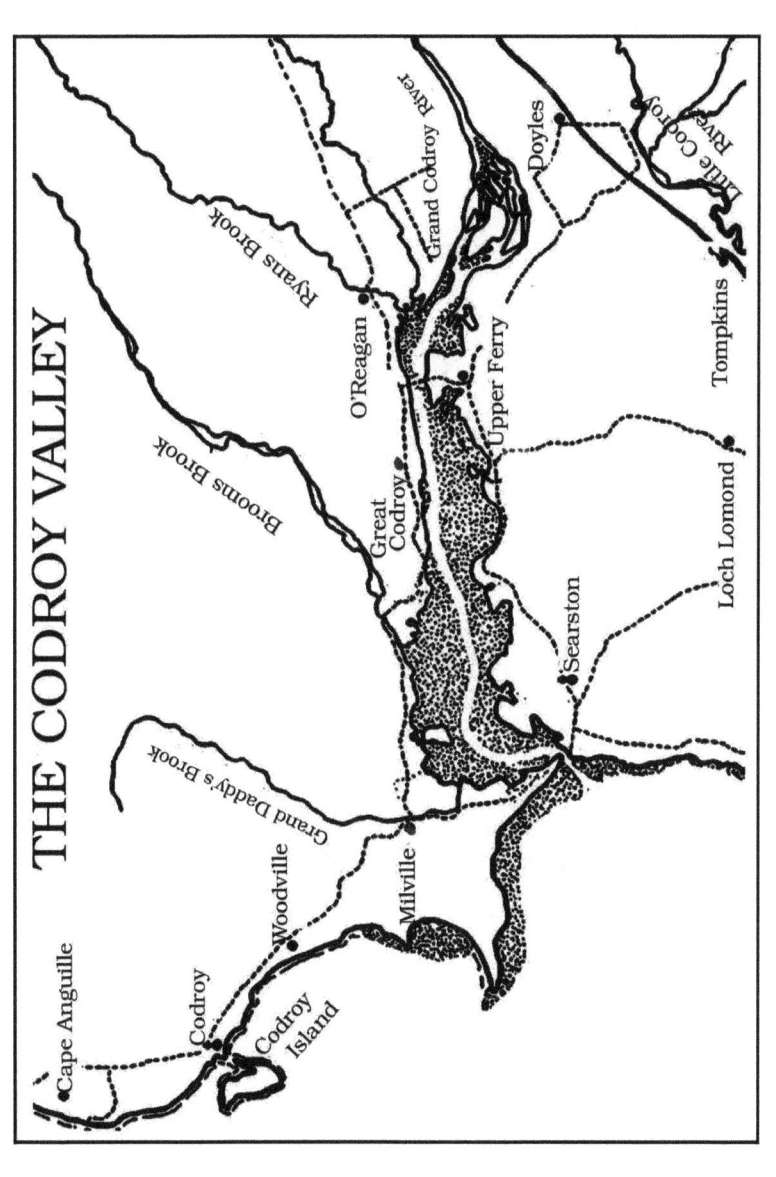

INTRODUCTION

Before the completion of the Trans-Canada Highway in 1966, the Codroy Valley on the west of Newfoundland tended to be regarded by outsiders as 'fairly remote'. To people who belong to 'out-of-the-way' places, however, such terms are irrelevant in a community that is complete in every way that matters to the folk who live there.

The Codroy Valley nestles between the Long Range Mountains and the Cape Anguille Mountains. It stretches inland following an alluvial plain between two rivers: the Grand Codroy to the north, and the Little Codroy to the south. To local folk it's always known as 'The Valley', as if there were no other valley in the world, far less Newfoundland. Breathtakingly beautiful as it is, the scenery is not what draws folk back – nor even the fishing and hunting, 'second to none'. It is the people who leave the most lasting impression.

To appreciate the way of life in any part of Newfoundland, however, visitors should bear in mind that, until 1949, Canada was another country. Anyone born before that year is, first and foremost, a Newfoundlander, belonging to a unique island with a long history that features the distinction of being Britain's oldest colony. Little wonder, then, that having grown up in the so-called 'remote' Hebrides of Scotland, I felt instantly at home among fellow islanders when I emigrated there in 1968. Given that Canada's newest province was less than twenty years old, it was very common to hear folk explain, 'I'm not a Canadian, I'm a Newfoundlander.'

This statement alone taught me that, to understand the social, cultural and historical context of a song, it is essential to appreciate where it comes from, and especially to acknowledge the people who compose and sing the song. On reflection, Gavin Sprott's statement about Scottish tradition equally applies to Newfoundland, 'If there is no land or work, there are no people, no livelihood, no stories, no music, no songs...'[1]

In the Codroy Valley, the folk who have worked on the land or fished the rivers and coastal waters for nearly two centuries are a mix of Irish, English,

---

[1] Gavin Sprott 'Traditional Music: The Material Background', (Cowan 1980) pp. 54–64.

Scottish Gaels, French and Mi'kmaq.² For as long as anyone remembers, they have enjoyed getting together for 'a few tunes', songs, yarns and a cup of tea. The kettle is always on the stove and, more often than not, a few glasses appear from the cupboard and make their way to the kitchen table. Come Friday night, there's sure to be a ceilidh or a kitchen party, with accordions, bagpipes, fiddles, guitars, spoons and mandolins as well as songs that would lift the heaviest heart. Then there's Saturday and Sunday too – you never run out of songs to sing or neighbours who'll stop by for a game of cards. ³

No need for an occasion; any time is good for a song, as I was to learn in 1968 when I first went there with a reel-to-reel tape recorder and a quest to record Scottish Gaelic songs for a graduate studies project at Memorial University of Newfoundland's Department of Folklore.⁴ The Codroy Valley, with its profusion of songs in three languages, turned out to be a folklorist's paradise that put me in mind of Hamish Henderson's comment when he first went to record songs in Scotland's berry-fields in the 1950s: 'It was like holding a tin can under the Niagara Falls.'⁵

Those old-fashioned kitchens, warmed by wood-stoves, still remain my all-time favourites, for no matter how fashions change, none can replace the atmosphere evoked there, or the comfort enjoyed. It was at one of those kitchen get-togethers, in the home of the late Anne Martin, that I first met Jerome Downey and his wife Rosie. The house, situated on the south end of the long bridge spanning the Grand Codroy River,⁶ is still a landmark, as are the white holiday cabins neatly strung out along the riverbank and

---

² Con Gabriel, first person I met in the Codroy Valley, was of Mi'kmaq extraction. He was my guide to the MacArthur household where I first began recording the Gaelic traditions of the area in 1968.

³ As the majority of settlers in the Codroy Valley were Roman Catholic, the relaxed attitude to Sunday was very different to my strictly Presbyterian Scotland upbringing in Skye, where any entertainment on Sunday was (and still is) out of the question. As for cards, to the older generation they were taboo on any day of the week!

⁴ The fieldwork recordings, deposited in Memorial University of Newfoundland Archives include contributions from individuals of French, Irish, English and Mi'kmaq backgrounds as well as Gaelic. Apart from the Gaelic recordings, most are unpublished except for a few examples in 'Scottish Gaelic, English, and French: Some Aspects of the Macaronic Traditions of the Codroy Valley, Newfoundland' in RLS (1972) pp. 25–30.

⁵ From Hamish Henderson's sleeve-notes on the recording, *The Berryfields of Blair*. Henderson (1919–2002) has an international reputation as poet and song-maker, as well as being Scotland's most important folksong collector and folklorist of the 20th century. It was his 1950s recordings (with Alan Lomax) of Scottish singers that first attracted Kenneth Goldstein to study with him in Scotland where he wrote his *Guide to Fieldworkers* and added momentum to his prolific output of recordings.

⁶ Built in 1926, this was the longest concrete bridge in Newfoundland. It was washed away, however, in January 1978. A new bridge has since been constructed.

frequented by tourists, fishermen and sportsmen.

Jerome's family lived on the opposite side of the river, on the same farm that had been home to the Downeys for several generations. The few miles of unpaved road was 'no distance at all' when it came to those kitchen 'times' and ceilidhs, for whenever there was a community or church event, Jerome would be invited to sing. When planning the annual regatta or the Codroy Valley Folk Festival, for example, folk would say, 'We'll need to ask Jerome,' as if there was only one Jerome in Newfoundland. Indeed, when it comes to singing, to folk in the Valley there *is* only one Jerome – Jerome Downey. As his nephew Hector MacIsaac put it: 'He's a man you don't meet every day.'[7]

---

[7] The line is from the song 'Jock Stewart,' which Hector sings as part of his own repertoire. It is also the title of a DVD and CD featuring Jerome's influence on Hector's career as a singer-song writer: *A Man You Don't Meet Everyday: Songs from the Codroy Valley,* (2007), hereafter cited DVD, 2007.

THE DOWNEYS

The north side of the grand Codroy River has been home to the Downey's since the early 1840s. The 1944 Census lists nine families of Downey's in the communities of O'Regan's and Great Codroy, among them, Jerome's parents, James and Teresa Downey and their family. James was born in the Valley in 1892, while Teresa (nee Wall), born in Harbour Main in 1896, moved to the Valley as a small child. Their first child Ed was born in 1916 and their second child Frances in 1917. By that time, James had cut the lumber and, with the help of a local carpenter, built the house that was to be the family home into the next generation. This was also the house in which the 1980 field recordings were made, for by then it had become home to Jerome, Rosie and their children.

James and Teresa's new two-storey house was similar to many that were built at that time: spacious, well-planned, with a large kitchen and living area, and several bedrooms upstairs. Like all homes, it was lit by kerosene lamps, as electricity did not come to the Valley until 1962. A wood stove was used for cooking, baking, heating water in a side-tank, and boiling the kettle for tea. The interior brick chimney radiated warmth to the upstairs, an enviable comfort when it came to bedtime during a long, harsh winter. A hole cut in the ceiling over the stove let the heated air rise to the rooms above and was a delightful eavesdropping station for children banished to bed early.[1]

To the little family of four (plus the respected grandfather ww Downey, who was honored with the bedroom at the top of the stairs) the new house may have seemed large; but not for long, as James and Teresa had ten more children, Mary (Sr. Andrina) in 1918, Bernard in 1920, Cecilia in 1921,

---

[1] In his book *Vernacular Architecture in the Codroy Valley (2002)*, Richard MacKinnon traces the evolution of several examples from this era. Most did not have a bathroom or even running water when they were built, and it was very common to see those amenities added in stages, as and when a family could afford to make such improvements. Joe recalls that his parents had running water installed in 1938 and in 1949, after Grandfather's room at the top of the stairs was no longer needed, the family installed a toilet, then, in 1951, a bath was added though they still had to carry hot water upstairs. When Jerome and Rosie moved in they gradually made improvements, while retaining the traditional style of the old house.

Jerome in 1923, Theresa in 1925, Anthony (Tony) in 1926, Kathleen in 1928, Joe in 1930, Anne in 1932, James in 1934, and Lucy in 1937. A large extension had been added to the house in the mid 1920s to accommodate the growing family.

Although the Census records James as the head of the household, James himself might have said that the true head of their household was Christ. James and Teresa, both devout Roman Catholics, brought up their children with unconditional love, care and discipline as well as sound spiritual guidance. The priest was central to all community activities and under his pastoral care most adhered to the values of the church. Children were baptized in infancy, and folk thought little of the long dirt road from Great Codroy to Searston as they attended mass or confession. Even on extremely stormy Sundays, James and his older boys would walk the five miles both ways to church.

The Downey's were not simply a "church once a week" family, but a family whose daily lives centered around prayer. Most families had a special time to recite the rosary (usually after the evening meal) but James' family waited until just before bed time. Every morning began with prayer, every meal began with grace. Every room in the house had a holy picture or a statue. Blessed medals and rosaries were given and received, so that no matter how far from home any might travel, there would be a silent reminder around the neck or in a pocket. James once saw a daughter off on the train with this checklist: "You have your ticket? You have your money? You have your rosary?"

Generations of philosophers (not to mention popular magazines) have offered advice on how to have a better lifestyle, but James and Teresa Downey had no need of such counsel. Providing food for the body, soul and mind came naturally to them, as did their attitude to hard work. Before they ever went to school, all the children would lend a hand, for even a little pair of hands can carry in firewood or help harvest potatoes. Each child had chores from milking to churning to gathering eggs, and each assumed responsibility equal to age for keeping the family fed and warm.

As schools had been a priority of the early priests, so too education was important in the Downey family. Laddu, the much-loved grandfather, taught the children to read before they ever started school. Evenings could be spent listening to family members read from a novel, having a spelling bee, or enjoying James recite the 'Inch Cape Rock'[2] or 'Horatius at the Bridge'[3]. Teresa was determined that her girls would have an education and, in due course, was satisfied that four went into nursing and three became teachers, suitable professions for the time and place. At one point in the late 1920s, the children were home schooled. Mary Burns, a cousin,

---

[2] Composed by the English poet Robert Southey (1774–1843), a contemporary and friend of Wordsworth and Coleridge.

[3] The 70 verses poem is by Thomas Babington Macaulay (1800–1859).

stayed for two years and she had "music". She played the organ (pump organs were in all the schools and many homes in the Valley), and she gave the beginning of musical training to the older children. Jerome's younger brother Joe recalls that the organ was a feature of family activities. With brothers and sisters in their teens when he was born, Joe looked back with affection on his early childhood.

> At that time we had an organ and the older ones of the family would be playing the organ – singing around the organ was a common thing in the house. And Jerome, I would have to say, was the best singer of the group.

As the older ones left the nest, their comings and goings opened up new worlds and new music. Theresa, the middle child, would bring home song sheets, such as "My Blue Heaven" or "Johnny Fedora", and Jerome, ever avid for songs, would have her play them over and over. The youngest boy James, who has shown considerable talent as a singer and a songwriter, also found Theresa an early support. During the war years, family sing a longs always featured Theresa playing and James singing, especially "Coming in on a Wing and a Prayer".

Radios became common in Valley homes during this period and the new songs and styles of singing were being assimilated into every kitchen gathering, becoming part of local repertoire. As Joe was only nine when war broke out and fifteen when it ended, I asked him what music he recalled during those years:

> The sounds of Lulubelle and Scotty, the Carter Family, Hank Snow, Wilf Carter (aka Montana Slim) seeped into the consciousness. A younger sister Anne at 79 can still make the hills ring with a yodel she learned at 14, and James (the brother) still plays guitar with an echo of his early love for Wilf Carter.[4] In those early days of radio, Jerome, with a young family to raise [in the early fifties], may not have had much time for selecting programmes, as his repertoire always seemed to reflect the more traditional songs and local compositions of the home-grown Valley songsters.[5]

Nevertheless, when recording songs for this collection, he surprised us by singing 'There's a Bridle Hanging on the Wall' and others which had been

---

[4] James died March 9, 2012. Also known as 'Jim', some of the many songs he composed were about the railway (reflecting his career as well as his passion). They are listed (along with the likes of Gordon Lightfoot's 'Railroad Trilogy') on http://www.railwaysongs.ca/ and can also be heard on the CD, Jim Downey, 'I Loved Working on the Railroad'.

[5] Correspondence Joe Downey, Feb. 2012.

stowed away in his memory, word-perfectly, all those years.

James and Teresa Downey were proud of their family. They considered their children gifts from God and were proudest of the two they "gave back", Bernard and Andrina. Bernard, who joined the Royal Canadian Air Force as a gunner, was killed when his plane crashed after a bombing run in February 1944. He is buried in Harrogate, England. To this day, his war medals and service photograph, forever age 23, are framed and displayed as a permanent reminder to the family and all who visit the Downey home. A visit with the family in 2004 proved to be no exception when Jerome quietly spoke of Bernard, recalling memories that six decades could not fade.

Mary Andrina was 'given back' in a different way. She joined the convent and became a music teacher. She claimed that she herself was not good to sing or good to play, but she could get people to sing together beautifully. She trained many award-winning choirs and had piano students until she turned eighty. Joe commented on Andrina's influence on society and younger siblings. "She taught music in schools in Corner Brook, Grand Falls, Stephenville, St. John's and so on – you see, the nuns always got moved. And on visits home, she also taught James, so he could read music (whereas Jerome couldn't – he just went by what he heard)."

Though it is now more than forty years since Teresa passed away, thirty years since James has passed, and the old house has been home to Jerome and Rosie since 1969, family members still talk of going home. To folk from the Valley, going home has always been important, no matter how far they travel to make a living, or how long it has been since they left. For many it's the highlight of the year. Even grandchildren who grew up thousands of miles from the Valley can be heard to say "any excuse is good" – Christmas time, special birthdays, wedding anniversaries, harvest time, no matter, so long as it's a chance to head home for the holidays. And no visit would be complete without songs, music, stories and laughter in a warm kitchen where time doesn't matter and the world's cares can be forgotten. "Come on Jerome! Just one more song!"

Jerome and Rosie on the wedding day, 1946 (top left).

In the front pew of St Anne's Church, Jerome (R) is ready to sing.

"You'd always sing at a wedding.... Then when someone else played, we'd have a waltz..." (Jerome and Rosie, 1990s).

Jerome (R) with one of his sons, sawing lumber on the hill behind their home (1980s).

Joe (L) and Jerome (L) outside the house built by their father, Great Codroy (1990s).

Jerome, centre stage at the Annual Codroy Valley Folk Festival with Bill Bruce (L) and Hector MacIssac (R), July 2006.

Jerome singing with Margaret Bennett, in his home, Great Codroy, 1980.

"I used to play for dances one time…." Jerome in 2007. (Top left)

"That's Bernard's photo and medals…" Rosie with Karen Farrell, 2007. (Top right)

Karen Farrell and Margaret Bennett with Jerome and Rosie, 2007. (Left)

The Downey family home, Great Codroy. (Bottom left)

Looking across the Grand Codroy River to the Downey's farm. (Bottom right)

THE SINGER AND THE SONG–MAKERS

JEROME – THE MAN HIMSELF

Within moments of being welcomed at the door, visitors to Jerome and Rosie's home have an immediate sense of family and community. Almost every wall displays framed photos of individuals, groups, events and celebrations spanning several generations. Each tells a story, like a picture exhibition set out for a guided tour, which Rosie willingly gives.

Jerome and Rosie were married in 1946, their first child was born in 1947 and their twelfth child in 1967. "Seven sons and five daughters, all grown up now," Rosie tells us, moving towards more recent photos. "And there's the grand-children – quite a few since you were here last… Some of them live near, but a good many come home for holidays. This year [2007] we had quite a few…"[1] Jerome is sitting by the window as Rosie leads us on a picture tour from the kitchen into the living room. "There were thirteen children in Jerome's family – he was the sixth, he was in the middle…"

'Middle child' stories are imagined myths to a man who remembers the advantages of having several siblings and a grandfather who lived with them: "He used to make snow-shoes, and he liked to sing when he worked. And we'd watch him weaving the hide in and out." Grandfather also told stories and taught them to read even before they went to school. Then, after he was gone, there were seven more brothers and sisters to share the house, the table, the chores, the rosary, the hymns and songs round the organ. The lid has been closed for "quite a while" and Rosie stands beside it as she explains, "This is not the organ they had then – the one that was here went to Frances. This one came from the *Family Herald*," (as if it just arrived, without bidding).

---

[1] Though I recorded Jerome in 1970 and then with Kenny Goldstein in 1980, the recordings quoted in this section were made on two more recent visits, October 28, 2006 and June 23, 2007. By then, Jerome and Rosie were in their mid-eighties and Jerome's health was failing as he had been diagnosed with Alzheimer's disease. (Recordings were made on mini-disc and, following a sudden microphone failure, on digital camera. Personal archive.)

Jerome smiles, as he joins the conversation: "Yes, we used to sing hymns to the organ, long time ago…"

"When would you do that?"

"Oh, almost any time at all – when the children would be young, you know. When we were kids."

"And did people keep the Rosary every night in your young day?"

Rosie replies emphatically, "Oh yes, yes, yes!" and I ask her, "Has that changed much?"

"Oh, I don't say there's very many of our children says the Rosary now. Some don't even go to mass. I'll tell you, though, they always went to mass when they were under our care. But then everything changed, and I don't see that anything's changed for the better – everything's changed for the worse! … I don't know where it's all going to go…"

"We'll just have to wait and see, I suppose," Jerome says, as Rosie points to a neat set of green books.

"Oh, yes, these are our Prayer Books…. And [on the top of the organ] that's Mother's hymn-book. Her name is in it, Mrs. James W. Downey. See," Rosie straightens up the loose pages, as 'Faith of Our Fathers' is about to fall out.

She lifts another music book saying, "It's got the Ave Maria. Jerome often sings that."

"So you sang in church, Jerome?"

"Oh yes!" they reply in unison, and for a moment Rosie looks surprised, as if to say "you surely knew that." She moves over to identify the nuns in a nearby picture. "That's my aunt and Joe Martin's aunt…"

I keep my eye on the nuns while asking yet another question:

"Jerome, did you ever sing 'Oh, Holy Night'?"

"I sung that a good many times!" he laughs, then immediately sings a few lines. Rosie takes a seat opposite, smiling with pleasure.

"We were third cousins, you know," she says, reciting connections that went back three generations. When Jerome joins the conversation, he addresses her as "My dear". There's a quiet gentleness between them and both are quick to smile. The roles are traditional, (like the ones I grew up with), so Rosie makes the tea, sets out the cups and home-baking, while Jerome stays with the visitors and continues the conversation. "Been a fine day… a lot of butterflies gather round that tree… I suppose the boys will get a moose license this fall… No, I haven't been cutting woods for a while, but I used to be always in the woods…. Nobody milking cows either…. My word, tape recorders are pretty small these days…"

It had been over thirty year since I first met Jerome and Rosie, but even in those days, in the best of health and full of energy, Jerome was not likely to tell you his life-story. He'd sing and play music till the cows came home, but why would anyone want to talk about their life? Unless maybe they were famous, and even then, you wouldn't go telling it yourself. As his nephew Hector MacIsaac said, looking back over his lifetime of sharing holidays and visits, there was never a time Jerome didn't sing. "His favourite way to communicate was to sing."[2]

Getting to know the singer is not necessarily about asking direct questions to find out what motivates him. Hearing one song may serve as an introduction to a singer's world, and perhaps the discovery that it is songs that make him tick. To the listener, the prime function of a song may be entertainment, but for the singer there are many others. There is a joy in singing that singers experience without attempting to analyse the feeling – that in itself would spoil it. Yet it is more than just the 'feel good factor', as some folk call it. Like the choruses of old songs, clichés about singing are well-worn: it can be for fun, for lifting the spirit, lightening the work or for bringing folk together, and, at times when words fail, only songs convey the inexpressible emotions of joy or grief.

Beyond the expression of emotion, songs may also articulate opinion. As with proverbs quoted as 'the wisdom of many and the wit of one', so it is with songs: there is a safe distance between speakers or singers and the audience. From a seemingly neutral ground, the singer gives voice to the sentiment of the song, which, if it is based on something controversial or local, may be of considerable advantage. If a listener happens to regard an expression as 'too close to the bone', there is acceptable 'out' for the singer: "It's just a song; if the cap fits..." and so on. For the song-maker, however, there may be no such 'out,' as songs will outlive the maker as long as there are singers to sing them.

In the four decades I have known Jerome, it seems that most of what I learned about him has been gained through songs and music. He himself said emphatically: "The greatest thing in the world, you know, is music. Oh heavens yes! I wouldn't be able to live without it! If the Lord made anything any better He kept it to Himself!"[3] Meanwhile, in sharing the context of that gift, Rosie has also played a role, adding to the experience and nurturing the friendship. Gradually I was to discover that it was not only friends or visitors who knew Jerome through his songs, but even his family. His brother Joe, who shared innumerable family get-togethers, remarked on how instantly Jerome came alive with song, and how much he cherished it:

> He loved getting together with Hector to sing... When Jerome and Hector get together everything else goes by the wayside, and it's music, music, the two of them feeding off each other...[over the years] I never knew a time when I'd be with him before and after a session with Hector... when he'd be anything but reveling in the time they spent together.

---

[2] DVD, 2007.
[3] MUNFLA 88-226.

One of Jerome and Rosie's granddaughters, Dale, who spent her life in the Valley, spoke for her generation. As they lived "only across the bridge,' the children would visit and stay overnight – "We loved that!" Looking back, she realized that the grandchildren too experienced Jerome through his and music. The house seemed filled with music and, at the end of the day, he could always sing you to sleep: "We'd stay over and very often and in the morning he'd be up early singing and playing the fiddle and there would be nothing for it then but everyone else had to get up!"

Jerome also played the button-box accordion, sometimes to accompany his own singing, or, if the occasion were a house party, he'd play for a waltz. "But years ago, when I was fifteen or sixteen, I used to play for dances all over the place here. Square dances, 'St Anne's Reel', 'Soldier's Joy' and 'The Little Burnt Potato' ... Oh, I used to play a lot of them. 'The Girl I left Behind Me', 'The Rakes of Kildare' – all them tunes..."[4] Completely self-taught, he held his fiddle at the angle that suited him, rather than in any textbook position. He didn't talk about how he played; he simply played. It was in singing, however, that he found his main expression and greatest audience response.

The sound of the singer's voice conveys much more than the lyrics and tune that comprise a song. And if, in Jerome's singing, we meet the man himself, then before long we also get to know his friends, neighbours, community and his philosophy of life. Alan Lomax, the world's most prolific song-collector observed that, "[t]he performer gives you his strongest and deepest feelings, and if he is a folk singer, this emotion can reveal the character of his whole community. ... Ask him how he does this, and he can no more tell you than a minister can tell you how to preach a sermon."[5] Lomax recognized the advantages of listening to, and recording, singers in their own environment, be it a farm or a factory, a fireside or a front-porch, a jail-house or a gas-station, with no imposed formality, no programme to follow and no anticipation of applause: "Folk song in a context of folk talk made a lot more sense than in a concert hall."[6]

Despite Jerome's immense popularity at local concerts, it was always in house visits, family gatherings, ceilidhs or kitchen parties that we met the man himself. In selecting songs from his vast repertoire, he shared his interests, aptitudes and values, as well as his warm sense of humour and his character. Jerome's whole life was punctuated by songs; "Oh, a lot o' songs! Never did stop to count them."[7] Neither did he stop to wonder

---

[4] Conversation with Heather M. MacDonald, recorded March 12, 1988, MUNFLA 88-226.

[5] Alan Lomax, 'Saga of a Folksong Hunter' (1960).

[6] *Ibid.*

[7] Unfortunately it did not occur to me (until it was too late) to make an inventory of Jerome's songs, which, had we counted them, would have undoubtedly numbered well over a hundred. The selection included in this collection was his choice of songs during the 1980 session, and represents only a fraction of the number he

where he got the songs; they were everywhere. Looking back over his life, however, 'everywhere' was within the family and community, and 'everyone' included his grandfather, his parents, siblings, friends and neighbours as well as voices he heard only on gramophone or radio.

Bearing in mind that Jerome was fifteen years old when Newfoundland had its first radio station,[8] and over twenty before radios appeared in the Valley, his earliest acquisition of songs was without any influence of media broadcasting. In those days, it was a big consideration for families to find money for gadgets such as a gramophone but, as Joe recalls, "a neighbour, Christina Jennings, had one,[9] then after Jerome and Rosie were married (1946) they moved into old Justin Downey's house, and there was one there." More than sixty years on, I asked Jerome about it:

MB: And did you listen to records as well – those old 78s?
Jerome: Oh, yes, yes, some of them.
MB: Did you have one of those players yourself?
Jerome: There was one in the house…you had to wind it up.
MB: And you had to have needles – remember, 'His Master's Voice' needles?[10]
Jerome: Yeah! (laughs)
MB: And do you remember any of the records you were listening to?
Jerome: Well, see, it was a long time ago.
[From other side of the room, Rosie agrees.]
MB: Did you have, say The McNulty Family[11] or John McCormack[12] or any of those?

---

actually knew. Some of the popular Newfoundland songs such as 'I'se the B'y' or 'The Star of Logy Bay' or 'The Squid Jigging Ground' may have seemed over-sung at the time we made the recording, and he purposely chose songs that Kenny may not have heard before. There was also the matter of time; there are only so many songs that can be sung in an evening.

[8] Song collector-merchant Gerald S. Doyle made the first broadcast in St. John's in 1932. It was not until 1939, however, that the Newfoundland Government established a radio station, BCN (Broadcasting Corporation of Newfoundland). CBC stations began broadcasting in 1949.

[9] The Jennings' house was more than a mile away from the Downeys.

[10] http://www.oldshopstuff.com/Shop/tabid/1248/ItemID/14750/Listing/Old–tin–His–Masters–Voice–loud–tone–needles/Default.aspx.

[11] The songs and music of this Irish American family were immensely popular and influential all over Newfoundland. Their records were among the first to be played on radio in Newfoundland, and 'Ma' McNulty's melodeon style was also influential among players. See Ted McGraw, 'The McNulty Family' (JSAM 2010), pp.451–473.

[12] Count John McCormack, as he became known, was born in 1884 and died in 1945. He was, and still is, regarded on both sides of the Atlantic as one of the greatest Irish tenors of two centuries.

Jerome: Oh, yes, [enthusiastically] I guess we did! We had some of them!

Who could forget the sheer vitality of the McNulties or the voice of great the John McCormack? The ethnomusicologist anticipating discussion at this point will be sorely disappointed at the missed opportunity of asking about musical influences and such. For the singer, that would have broken the spell; the magic of a remembered voice would be gone in an instant. At the very mention of 'The Rose of Tralee', 'When Irish Eyes are Smiling', 'Kathleen Mavourneen', the sheer pleasure of McCormack's singing seemed to flood back. We can almost hear the 'sob' in his voice, as between us we rhyme them off. Now it is Jerome's turn to discover 'new' information when I tell him: "My paternal grandfather was from County Armagh... John Bennett. He had a good voice... just loved McCormack." Meanwhile, I completely forgot to ask Jerome what happened to the wind-up gramophone.[13]

The wireless, as everyone called the radio, came later, "around the mid-forties." As in Ireland and Scotland, its appearance in most homes was hastened by anxiety over Second World War news reports. Even then, they were all operated by large cell-batteries, to be used sparingly and not "blaring in the background all day long" (as my mother would have it). Jerome was 38 years old when the Valley was connected to an electricity supply, and nearly 40 when television edged into most houses. As his old friend Allan MacArthur once said, "When the television came in the front door, the *sgeulachdan* [story-telling] went out the back."

During my 2006 visit, when I happened to pick up one of our conversations with, "Remember old Allan MacArthur?" Jerome lit up. "Oh, yes, a fine old man. Kind of a saint, well, he really was. I think he loved everybody and everybody loved him... Now he had lots of songs – mostly Gaelic, but some in English... but he never gathered up so many as I did 'cos he was getting older by the time he started to sing in English... He's been gone a long time now, quite a while..."[14] Over forty years, in fact, and in all that time, this was as close as Jerome ever got to making any comment about the extent of his own song repertoire.

To most singers, there is no need to analyse the process of acquiring songs; the fact that we sing is evidence enough. Singers are aware, however, of a myriad of factors that contribute to the acquisition of songs and their

---

[13] Jerome and Rosie moved back into the old family homestead in 1969 by which time 12 inch 33 rpm vinyl records had taken over from 78 rpm's and electric radiograms and record players had become a common feature of most homes.

[14] In 1959 Kenneth Peacock recorded songs in both English and Gaelic from Allan MacArthur (then in his mid-seventies), see *Songs of the Newfoundland Outports*, (1965, Vol. 3). Between 1968 and 71, I recorded over twenty Gaelic songs from him, though none in English. See *Dileab Ailean: The Legacy of Allan MacArthur* (2010).

performance, such being rocked to sleep to the sound of a lullaby or, more formally, being taught by a music teacher.[15]

All of these imply the need to listen carefully, for without that, there is little chance of learning. Jerome was clearly a good listener, not only to songs, which he seemed to absorb rather than learn, but also to the spoken word. His training was not anything he, or his generation, was aware of; it was simply a way of life. As in similar social settings in Ireland and Scotland, nobody seemed in awe of the concentration span of a child listening to an epic, such as the seventy-verse "Horatio at the Bridge" recited in the Downey household.

In recognizing that our sense of what is 'ordinary' can vary as widely as our experience of life, we might appreciate that, in an environment where no one recites poetry, the very activity may seem extraordinary.[16] In a world where the concentration span of the 'average' person is measured in sound bites of so many seconds, shadows of doubt might even be cast over the claim of Jerome's generation to the number and length of items they committed to memory. To avoid bias, I invited opinion from an elderly friend, Nan Doig, who, like Jerome, came from a large family, and grew up on a hill-farm, in a house without electricity. As she had not long celebrated her hundredth birthday, it seemed apt to record Nan talking about life in rural Scotland.[17] She had lived through two world wars, thought nothing of the "miles we had to walk to school" and explained how "Everybody helped on the farm. And everyone made their own entertainment... Duncan played the accordion...."

"And did any of your folk recite poems," I ask, "For example, 'The Inchcape Rock' or any others?"

"Oh yes, there was a lot of that... mind you, that poem wasn't one we got in school. I just heard it... a long, long time ago... it wasn't one I used to recite myself," she said, then quoted the last verse:

> But even in his dying fear,
> One dreadful sound could the Rover hear;
> A sound as if with the Inchcape Bell,
> The Devil below was ringing his knell.

---

[15] As a singer, I am generally cautious of any analysis that does not resonate with the singer's own experience, however well founded in observation or behavioral psychology it may claim to be. This discussion is therefore based on contributions from Jerome, his family, friends and other singers who share his experience of life or of singing.

[16] As Scottish poet Alexander Hutchison point out, however, it is a feature nowadays of 'performance poetry' events. [Email, 2012].

[17] Conversation with Nan Doig (b. 1912), Comrie, Perthshire, May 2012. Between 2010 and 2012, I also recorded Nan extensively for an oral history project, 'Perthshire Memories', archived at the School of Scottish Studies, University of Edinburgh and the Perth and Kinross Archive, Perth.

"There's a good lesson there,"[18] she laughed. "You wouldn't ever forget that and when you learn it young, it stays with you for life." Like Jerome, Nan presumes the poem to be so well known that the lesson goes without saying – to both of them, it is obvious: If you do something out of spite or malice, you may perish on your own 'rock'.

There seems also to be a 'lesson' in how individuals perceive what they term as 'normal' or 'ordinary' regarding what we commit to memory and retain in an active or passive repertoire. Some aspects may relate to a particular generation, or point in history, (such as 'in our time'), others may have a connection to education or geographic location. Nevertheless, our general perception seems to be more a product of the social setting of our lives and the culture with which we identify.[19] Despite living much of my life outside of Gaelic Scotland, where I grew up and was schooled (in English), I can acknowledge that cultural 'norms' accepted in childhood may wield more influence on my life than the later 'higher education' attained outside of that society. As a product of a culture, rather than of a place, establishment, time or generation, it therefore seemed natural for me to feel 'at home' in Jerome's 'ordinary' world, where 'everyone' sang or recited.[20] Regardless of how 'ordinary' he may have seen himself, however, Jerome was no ordinary singer.

STYLE AND REPERTOIRE

What is it about a voice, a singing style or the ability to capture an audience that all add up to what is recognized as 'star quality'? Given his uncanny instinct in that field,[21] if only he were still with us, Kenny

---

[18] A loud bell, to warn ships of danger, is attached by a rope to Inchcape Rock, a notoriously perilous island off the coast of Scotland. When Rover, a villain who cares for nobody, severs the rope, ships strike the rock and sink, creating untold grief to all who lose loved ones. Later, in a dreadful storm, Rover himself perishes when his own ship hits the rock.

[19] It was accepted as 'normal' that every school day began with the recitation of a Bible verse (homework from previous day) so that in the course of a year children accumulated complete chapters, the 'Shorter Catechism', poems, passages from Shakespeare as well as English and Gaelic songs for the school choir. At home, my sisters and I had Gaelic songs from our mother, Scots from our father, and, with our grandparents, immersion in the culture of the Gael that was simply our way of life.

[20] For further discussion on the shared 'song experiences' of the Codroy Valley and the Highlands and Islands of Scotland, see M. Bennett, "'A Song for Every Cow She Milked...' Sharing the Work and Sharing the Voices among the Gaels" (*Sharing the Voices: The Phenomenon of Singing VI: Proceedings of the International Symposium*, 2010).

[21] Among Kenny's groundbreaking recordings was one of the Clancy Brothers and Tommy Makem – a 12-inch LP with sleeve notes – and the rest is history. In a

Goldstein would have been the ideal person to respond. On the uncut fieldwork recordings, Kenny's energy, lively enthusiasm and appreciation are unmistakable, as much 'preserved for posterity' as the songs and the qualities that emerge in Jerome's singing.

A 'good voice' may be described in terms of being melodic, tuneful, flexible, warm, resonant, and so on. Nevertheless, possessing such a voice does not necessarily qualify the singer to be known as 'a good singer'. More curiously, a singer can have an out of tune, technically 'bad' voice, yet may be regarded as 'a good singer'.[22] Jerome, however, was clearly blessed with a good voice and, from boyhood, was known as one of the finest singers in the Valley.[23] Listeners sense that he has a 'presence' about him that reflects a deep connection to his songs. His delivery or performance may seem so natural that the listener scarcely notices his outstanding breath control that gives him enormous scope to interpret a song. Rather than disrupt a line or a sentence with an intake of air, Jerome could effortlessly sing an entire verse in one breath, if that is what makes best sense of the meaning. Singers who seem to spend their lives working on phrasing and breath control may envy his capacity to retain that breath; even across a natural pause or musical 'rest' it never becomes an excuse for a quick gasp of air.

There may be few singers in the world better qualified to discuss Jerome's style of singing than the legendary Cathal McConnell from County Fermanagh who grew up in a dynasty of traditional Irish singers and musicians.[24] Despite decades of travelling the world with 'The Boys of the Lough' and also as a solo singer and virtuoso flute-player, Cathal is as much at home by the fireside as he is on the world stage. Equally

---

tribute to Kenny, Stephen Winick, (Folklorist and writer at the American Folklife Center at the Library of Congress) wrote, 'As a fieldworker and a record producer, the work he did during the 1950s and early 60s alone made him a towering figure in the folk music revival.' Winick, a former graduate student who was inspired by Kenny's teaching, also listed seminal records of Kenny's, including Ewan MacColl and A.L. Lloyd, Lucy Stewart, Jean Ritchie, the Rev. Gary Davis, Sara Cleveland and blues singer Lightnin' Hopkins. See Steve Winick (sic), 'Kenneth S. Goldstein, 1927–1995' (*Dirty Linen*, 1996).

[22] With hesitation, and admiration, I'd suggest anyone looking for an example to analyse might listen to Lee Marvin singing 'I Was Born Under a Wandering Star'.

[23] Outside the Valley Jerome achieves recognition largely through his nephew, Hector MacIsaac, who widely acknowledges Jerome to be the main influence on his career as a singer.

[24] Cathal's long career began in 1962 when he won the All-Ireland championship in both flute and whistle. In 1967 he was one of the founders of the 'Boys of the Lough' and is now the only member of the original group. In 2010 Cathal was honoured with one of Ireland's most prestigious awards for traditional singing, the Gradam Ceóil ("esteem for music"), presented by the Irish Gaelic television channel TG4. See also, *I Have Travelled This Country: Song of Cathal McConnell*, (with DVD, 2011).

loved in Scotland, where he has lived for over forty years, Cathal is always keen to listen to other singers and new songs. After listening intently to the recording of Jerome, Cathal had this to say:

> I never heard him before in me life but I'm very impressed ...I can picture him in me mind, a big, country man. He's obviously a very, very natural singer. He knows his own style, and it just flows, it's so casual. He makes difficult singing sound easy... [what strikes me about him is] his long phrasing ... very good breath control. I'm quite amazed... there's examples in Ireland, like Brigitte Tunney, Paddy Tunney's mother, singing 'As I Roved Out'. And she sang a long phrase – he demonstrates first the line – by-line phrasing and then sings a two-line phrase in one breath] – it's very difficult to do. Jerome's singing is effortless and melodic; he's an outstanding singer, a singer's singer. When you listen to this man you get an insight into something that's older and very valid... Definitely, without question, he's a singer's singer.[25]

When Christopher Underwood, Professor of Singing at Royal Conservatoire of Scotland, listened to the recording of Jerome, he had this to say:

> He represents one of the great strengths of traditional folk singing, which comes from a real individual. We hear through his voice the events of his life and a strong sense of character imbues all he sings. His voice has a strength and natural resonance...[26]

As with Cathal, Jerome's approach to singing shows remarkable focus, not only in his singing but also in his listening, as every word matters to him. A 'parrot fashion' style of repetition is alien to him, for, just as in storytelling, the entire piece has to make sense. Jerome was perfectly capable of reproducing lyrics exactly as they were written, such as with 'The March of the Cameron Men'; but as often as not there was no print version of a song. He would therefore absorb it as if it were a story, occasionally modifying a word or line to make better sense.

In 'The Galway Shawl', for example, folk who know the song will catch the 'change' to the first line, usually sung "In Oranmore in the County Galway". Yet only people familiar with that part of Galway would know of the existence of that little village. And so Jerome sings 'Erinmore', which has sounds like it is rooted in Ireland. As Hamish Henderson said of the great ballad singer Jeannie Robertson, who had a similar approach, Jerome displayed 'active participation' in the songs he chose to sing.[27]

---

[25] Recorded in Edinburgh, June 2012.

[26] Correspondence, Prof. C. Underwood, July 2012.

[27] See, Hamish Henderson, 'The Ballad, the Folk and the Oral Tradition' pp. 65–101 in Edward J. Cowan (ed). *The People's Past*, p. 69.

At times, for the sake of amusement, or 'sheer devilment' (pronounced 'divilment'), Jerome surprises his audience with slight changes to allude to an 'in joke' or to make some subtle point (we may only guess). He sings directly to his audience, whether it be only one or two people or a big crowd. As he has always performed locally, he has the advantage of knowing most, if not all, of his audience. In watching Jerome's facial expression as he sang, as well as listeners' response, there seems little doubt that textual changes became one of his ways of staying connected to his those present.[28]

If there happened to be an opportunity to catch listeners off guard, Jerome would take advantage to good effect. Two of the songs in this collection stand out as examples of the dynamics between singer and listener, in both instances the sudden changes are intended for amusement. He sang 'I Am a Roving Peddler' early in the session, and then later, Kenny asked him to sing it again. (He may have detected some extraneous noise and wanted a better recording.) In the first version Jerome sang the phrase 'where the charming women dwell' but on the second 'take' that line became 'where the great big women dwell', sung with more gusto and suppressed laughter.[29]

In 'The Bachelor's Lament', Jerome sang a verse where, much to the amusement of his audience, he would name one of the women in the company, catching her out unexpectedly. Occasionally, when the very suggestion of a young woman eyeing up this old bachelor made a teenage girl or newly married woman blush with embarrassment that could cause even more mirth. Such was the case when we visited Jerome with Karen Farrell, the young wife of a former neighbour. Everyone knew that Karen and Brian had been going steady since she was in her teens, and he was her only boyfriend. So, on the first 'take' Jerome sang, "There's Karen Farrell watching me, she's the devil for the boys!" On the second, he completely took me by surprise by singing, "Now there's Margaret Bennett watching, she's the devil for the boys!" Happily we all laughed, particularly Kenny.

Jerome's sense of timing was one of the features that characterized his performance and delivery, not only in his songs but also in his stories. For that reason, his short anecdote about Paul E. Hall is included, complete with the lead-up of general conversation and Kenny's questions. On the surface, it is 'only' about a man who dresses up in his Sunday suit on a weekday, so when Jerome meets him he asks if there is a special occasion. But listen to his impeccable timing; the pauses are as crucial as the text. In this sense also Jerome was both gifted and intelligent, finely tuned to his audience as well as to the story or song. (Pay attention, singers, for herein

---

[28] Newfoundland folklorists George J. Casey, Neil V. Rosenberg and Wilfred W. Wareham discuss the subject in their article, 'Repertoire Categorization and Performer-Audience Relationships: Some Newfoundland Folksong Examples', (*Ethnomusicology* 1972), pp. 397–403.

[29] This collection retains the first take on this song and the second take on 'The Bachelor's Lament'.

lies the secret of the singer who can hold an audience regardless of the song or the story it tells.) In Jerome's singing we begin to understand the meaning of the maxim, "Timing can be everything".

Acquiring a song repertoire is dependent on taste, personal choice, aptitude and enthusiasm as well as cultural and social setting. It cannot simply be a matter of family environment, for within the same generation, tastes may vary widely. As the youngest of four singing siblings with an age-range of two and a half years (twins in the middle), I became aware from an early age that, despite shared surroundings, not all siblings shared taste in song or for unaccompanied singing. And this was also the case in Jerome's family, with individual repertoires developing accordingly.

Kenneth S. Goldstein discussed 'repertory' in terms of a singer's personal history as well as relationship with the audience,[30] which, on this occasion, consisted of only four people. Jerome's rapport with his listeners was immediately evident and the songs he sang largely reflected his own choice. Occasionally a question or topic in general conversation reminded him of a song which he then sang. In all, there were twenty-three songs, which, for those inclined to classify, consisted of ten local compositions (mostly satires); three broadside ballads (or variants); three Country and Western songs; two Newfoundland songs (composed outside the Valley); two music-hall songs; (or variants); one 'concert' song learned at school[31]; and one classic (Child) ballad. Singers might view them in terms of a set list, and, apart from the omission of any sacred songs, they can fairly be said to represent the eclectic mix that comprised Jerome's repertoire. The range also fits accurately with his brother Joe's observation that Jerome's selections "always seemed to reflect the more traditional songs and local compositions of the home-grown Valley songsters."[32]

In 2007 when I asked Jerome if he had a favourite song, his response resonated with the experience of many singers: "I did have a good many favourite songs through the years, but then sometimes your favourite song gets left behind." Whether we sing or not, songs relate to our lives. They become closely associated with particular times, people, places, events, even exact moments, such as when and where we first heard a song – "They're playing our song!" – or the voice that first sang it – "and nobody can sing it like that". As life moves on, a favourite song can get 'left behind'

---

[30] See, Kenneth S. Goldstein, 'On the Application of the Concepts of Active and Inactive Traditions to the Study of Repertory' (*JAF* 1971), pp. 62–67.

[31] The only song that does not fit the other categories is 'The Cameron Men', which is seldom heard outwith the concert platform, as few untrained singers can master it.

[32] In his article 'Newfoundland Vernacular Song' Peter Narvaez discusses aspects of song selection and repertoire as a reflection of Newfoundland culture. (*Popular Music* 1995) pp. 215–219.

sometimes without being noticed, and, once in a while, intentionally. If a song begins to evoke pain, it's time to move on. Very soon, however, another song comes along with the kind of impact that motivates the singer to learn it.

LEARNING A SONG

Singers often introduce a song by telling where they got it, or from whom they learned it – otherwise, someone is sure to ask: "Where did you get that song?" Such was Jerome's style – it was second nature to him to acknowledge song-makers and folk who shared their songs. It was a new experience for Jerome, however, when, after he had sung Hughie O'Quinn's composition, 'The Sealers' Song', Kenny asked *how* he learned that particular song. The dialogue between folklorist and singer bears transcription as it sparked off a discussion that could go on for some time to come:

KG: Now, that was written by Hughie O'Quinn?
Jerome: Yes.
KG: How long ago did he write that?
Jerome: Oh, Wednesday night, March 17, 1965.
KG: And how did you learn this song?
Jerome: Oh, just hear 'em once and then I sing them.
KG: My God! To sing a song that long? [eleven verses]
Jerome: Oh yes.
KG: Go on, you're putting me on!
Jerome: Well, I couldn't do it now, but back then I used to learn them, once was enough –
KG: First of all you're not that old –
Jerome: No, that's when I learned that, I mean, that would be away back, years ago, a long way back. So –

There was scarcely a split-second pause, when Kenny moved on and asked if Jerome knew any other songs by Hughie – happily he did, and nothing more was said as they seemed to 'agree to disagree'. Their exchange raises some interesting issues, however, as Jerome was clearly as surprised by Kenny's disbelief as Kenny was by Jerome's claim to learn a song 'at one go'. To singers, however, in Jerome's account of how he learned a song there may be more reason for envy than doubt, if we consider what other discussants have to say about the subject.[33]

---

[33] Folklorist Edward D. Ives, who was also a folk singer, discussed the subject with singers and song-makers he extensively recorded in Maine, New Brunswick and

As the intervening years may have sucked us into the world of 'click and search', singers become aware that their approach to learning songs may also be undergoing changes. Undoubtedly there are advantages to be enjoyed in new technology, including (in this case) being able to discuss the question via email.[34] Opting for an informal approach, I got in touch with fourteen folk (friends acquainted with, or part of the 'traditional music scene'), all of whom knew Kenny personally or through his recordings. They were invited to express an opinion on the transcription of the conversation, if possible based on actual experience and consider the question: Is it possible to be able to sing a song after hearing it only once?

All fourteen responded immediately, but among them, only one (on the Irish-American circuit) emphatically disagreed, advising me 'Jerome was pulling your leg'. Two (both urban Scots) had no opinion as to whether it is humanly possible, but their own experience was one of continued repetition; three (two urban Scots, one English) had a few examples, both personal and observed, to support Jerome's claim, though most said they would need to hear the song three or more times; eight (six rural Scots, one urban Scot, one American resident in Scotland) agreed it was entirely possible, adding actual examples to support their opinions.

Poet and playwright George Gunn singled out Hamish Henderson as a remarkable example, encountered when he first got to know his fellow 'makker', also a singer and folklorist:

> I mind Hamish telling me – in fact I've seen him listening to things and he just had them [stored in his memory]. He had that facility; I don't think he had much technique about it, but he just had the gift…he could quote huge amounts of stuff to me that I'd ask him about and [as it was totally without notice] he'd never researched it, he'd never … [consciously learned it] – that was the thing about Hamish, whatever he learnt, he had a gift for that, and I think that stood him in good stead. I remember another time, asking him about [a fairly obscure subject I was working on] and Hamish, from some little compartment in his brain, just opened up, and out it came, the whole thing. I said, "That saves me a trip to the National Library of Scotland!"[35]

Prince Edward Island. In particular, see, *Larry Gorman, the Man Who Made the Songs* (1964) and *Joe Scott: The Woodsman Songmaker* (1978). From his interviews with woodsmen, Ives concluded (pp. 396–98) that most said they would need to hear the song two or three times to be sure of it.

[34] As three people were available for a 'round the table discussion' their opinions were recorded. (March 2012, used with permission).

[35] Recorded in Thurso, March 31, 2012. The conversation includes an anecdote from the mid-1980s, recalling Hamish reciting Walter Scott's ballad 'Glenfinlas' (more than 60 verses) which he knew as a teenager.

Fellow poet Adam McNaughtan, (best known for his outstandingly witty songs), could also relate to Jerome's remark, though his own experience was different. Looking back over the years, he reflected:

> I certainly learned words more quickly in my youth than I do now. I have no songs in my *current* repertoire that I learned at one hearing. Songs that I learned [this way] were either short, or simple and repetitive; by the time I sang them in public I would have heard them more than once. (In the early days of folk clubs there were few songs that you only heard once) Also when I did sing such a song, it turned out that the tune was different and the words had changed.

Gordeanna McCulloch, whose recordings of the 'muckle sangs' (big ballads) have travelled the world, said she took 'a fair while' to learn one, but added:

> ...unless it's a very short song – like 'Kissin's Nae Sin'. I usually have to go over and over the words to bed them in. Wish I could sing a song after just one listening, 't would be like magic. Another thing I do after learning a song is (unconsciously) change the words – how this happens I don't know. Maybe something to do with whatever feels, sits, tastes right in the mou'...

A friend of Kenny's since the late Fifties (when he recorded her Aunt Lucy), Elizabeth Stewart also said that it was something she occasionally did, "but it wouldn't have to be a very long song – you could do it by working on the story, and what its all about."[36] And, in recalling Norman Kennedy's learning of a song ('The Sweet Primroses') after hearing it only once, Pete Shepheard thought it was achievable because "it is one of those songs where the narrative flows very well." Though Pete himself "learned it from Norman by writing out the text from a recording of him singing it," he considered tunes to be "another matter":

> I have a very good memory for tunes and an ability to improvise tunes in a traditional form. At the age of six I came home from being at a performance of the Pirates of Penzance and was happily singing the tunes – I can still remember the occasion.

Though opinions on the 'Jerome–Kenny conversation' were invited individually (by email), there was a curiosity as to what others experienced. Tom Mckean of the Elphinstone Institute in Aberdeen, whose folklore

---

[36] Elizabeth's biography and repertoire, compiled and edited by Alison McMorland, contains 145 songs. *See, Up Yon Wide and Lonely Glen: Travellers' Songs, Stories and Tunes of the Fetterangus Stewarts,* (2012). Elizabeth recalls her Aunt Lucy being recorded by Kenny Goldstein in 1959–60.

fieldwork has taken him into the company of both Gaelic and Scots singers, considered it to be "absolutely possible". He cited three examples of singers of traditional Scots songs, (Gordon Easton, Norman Kennedy and Willie Mathieson of Ellon) whose youthful success may have been due to a familiarity with the vocabulary and frameworks of traditional songs, then concluded with a request: "Tell us more about this [Jerome] project."

Responses from the Gaelic tradition were also positive, with singers Margaret Callan (from North Uist) and Margaret Stewart (from Lewis) referring to old-style singers for whom it was not unusual to learn a song after one hearing. Also, having grown up in the Outer Hebrides in the 1940s, Bill Innes recalled two old men who claimed to be able to re-tell a long story word for word after one hearing – Duncan MacDonald from South Uist, and Angus MacMillan (1874–1954) from Benbecula.[37] He sent his translation (from Gaelic) of the eulogy written by folklorist Calum Maclean when they died within weeks of each other:

> I spent more than three years on Angus's tales alone. There were only 165 of them but I had to write 10,000 pages of manuscript before we had run our course. Duncan's longest story *'Sgeulachd Mhanuis'* took an hour and a half to tell. The longest one of Angus's, about *Alasdair Mac a' Cheird*, took nine hours to tell! There were another 43 that took more than three hours ...

The earlier discussion with George Gunn was joined by two singer-songwriters, Nancy Nicolson and Dick Gaughan, who could also identify with Jerome's experience – Nancy in observing others, and Dick from his own experience:

MB: Do you think it's possible just to hear a song once and then sing it?
Dick: Yes. I used to do it when I was younger. I had the trick of doing that – I couldn't do it now; the memory doesn't retain things quite as it did. It's a concentration thing. I don't quite have the concentration that I had. It was something that could be learned if you practised. I certainly remember learning a song on one hearing. I couldn't give you exactly word for word but what I could remember is enough of the story and enough of the song to be able to reconstruct the song later on. And I had that probably until I was in my thirties.
MB: Did it make a difference, for example, if you went to a quiet space

---

[37] In 1949 Calum Maclean (folklorist with the Irish Folklore Commission) and John Lorne Campbell recorded ballads and stories from both men as well as other storytellers, notably, the famous Angus MacLellan (Aonghus Beag). He also claimed to hear be able to tell a 'short' story after one hearing though longer tales (lasting for hours) would take several hearings. See John Lorne Campbell's *'Introduction'* to *Stories from South Uist*, 1960, pp. vii–xi. The web archive *Tobar an Dualchais* has on-line recordings of all their voices.

and you just went over the story in your head, say, by the time you got home, just going over it in your head?

Dick: I would need to play it back to myself a few times to reconstruct it, but I certainly had it. I'll tell you who else had it with tunes, is Cathal McConnell. You could play McConnell a tune once and he had it... And Martyn [Bennett] did it. It's a thing you can learn. And I learned it when I was a kid... If you think about it, the whole bardic tradition would have been based on that. Part of being a bard would have been that ability to remember and invent things in their head. You remember all kinds of triggers; I mean there's all kinds of tricks to do that. As I say, I couldn't do it now cos I don't have the concentration any more. You know, I'd have to hear a song two or three times now.

MB: Would it have to be a song that grabbed you?

Dick: Oh yes, yes. It would be that strong, I *want* this song. [laughs][38]

Aside from his formidable reputation as a singer and flute-player, Cathal McConnell is also known for his modesty and generous spirit, shown in his response to Gaughan's assertion and the original question:

Cathal: I remember a session one night there was a man called Francie Quinn – he just died lately – and he played these two reels. And I was young at the time, about nineteen, a long time ago. And one was a three-part reel called 'Munco Hill' and the other was a four-part reel called 'The Spike Island Lasses', and I *wanted* these tunes. Well I had them right enough – and Francie and I often talked about that.

MB: And was there ever a time when you learnt a song in one go?

Cathal: No, no, not at all. When I go to learn a song I write it down first, and then after I start to sing it at various social occasions, bars, and the likes, and then I'd be sure of it...I'd sing it at a concert. But Eddie Butcher[39] would have learnt a song very quickly when he was younger, and he might have had that facility when he was younger....but there's a story told about Eddie Butcher's father, about 1920 or so. I presume he *heard* of the song so went to hear this song being sung because he could neither read nor write so there was no point writing it out for him. It's a song called 'The Trader', it's about a ship going down somewhere off the coast of Ireland – it's eight or nine verses, quite a long song. And this man who was a school-master sang it for Eddie's father, and after the

---

[38] Recorded in Thurso, March 13, 2012.

[39] Traditional singer Eddie Butcher (1900–1980) from Co. Derry also composed songs. He had a repertoire of approximately 300 songs (several of which Cathal sang) and was one of Irelands's most influential singers.

song he said to him "Do you want to hear it again?" and he said, "No, I already have it."

In the old times people had to rely on their memories for both the words and the tunes and it was a very sophisticated skill.[40]

Returning to the Valley in 2012, there was no need to raise the question (or the controversial conversation) with folk who had grown up hearing Jerome sing – the very mention of his name set the records straight. As folk in the Valley prepared for a celebration of Jerome at the 2012 Codroy Valley Folk Festival, Joe Bruce, who also sang in the church choir beside him, looked back with admiration:

Joe B: I've sat at the table across from Jerome many a time, with a jug of fine grog, and sang.
MB: When I first heard Jerome I thought there must be few singers could match Jerome Downey. Is that an exaggeration?
Joe B: No, it's not. And Jerome didn't need any accompaniment. Jerome could do his own thing and it just came naturally to him. He had a wonderful voice and a good memory and a great delivery for songs. He could just hear a song once, and if he wanted that song he remember it. That's a trait that Jerome had. He could hear it and he got it, and that didn't matter if it was something that someone was singing at a festival or something that was going on in your church choir – the Director went through it *once* and Jerome had it!

Considering that Jerome sang for over eighty years, it almost goes without saying that keeping his repertoire alive was also important to him. As he explained to Heather MacDonald:

> If anybody sings, you know, they gotta sing a certain amount every day to keep themselves ... and same with the violin... you lose it if you don't... And you gotta sing a song at least once a year if you're going to remember the words of it."[41]

In the world of singers, as long as we have breath, we sing, for songs are the life-force of singers; without them our world may become meaningless and silent.

---

[40] Recorded in Edinburgh, June, 2012
[41] MUNFLA 88-226.

LOCAL SONGS, WORDSMITHS AND TUNE-FINDERS

Jerome's sense of community and place is strongly reflected in the fact that half the songs he chose to sing for this collection were composed in Newfoundland. As well as having Newfoundland songs popularized by recording artists such as John White, Joan Morrissay and Dick Nolan, Jerome also had several more songs composed in the Valley, which will hopefully be noted by other collectors. Across the island, acquiring a repertoire such as this may not seem unusual, as several radio programmes featuring Newfoundland performers were a regular source of songs. So also was the weekly CBC television show, 'All Around the Circle', which ran between 1964 and 1975. As anyone who saw it knows, in those days every eye was on the set; when there was a chorus to join nobody needed inviting, and when the band played a jig, it was not unusual for floor rugs be rolled back as step-dancers or sets took to the floor.[42]

Reflecting on the wide range of songs to be found in Newfoundland, Herbert Halpert remarked:

> The lively folksong tradition in Newfoundland has preserved a large body of traditional songs along with an equally great number of theatre and popular songs. But more than that, Newfoundlanders have had an extraordinarily vigorous tradition of composing new song texts... that are sung to traditional tunes.[43]

Often, as soon as one such composition was sung it could take off, leaving the name of its composer behind as it entered oral tradition. Such is the case in the Codroy Valley where not all the wordsmiths can now be identified and, in some cases, others chose not to be. Of those represented here, Jerome knew three of them well – Paulie Hall, Hughie O'Quinn and Micky Jim MacNeil. Three very different characters, they not only spent time in Jerome's company and enjoyed his friendship, but also recognized his importance to their craft. As Jerome's nephew Hector MacIsaac aptly recalled:

> Just hanging around with [Jerome] it became clear that he was the conduit through which these song-writers in the Valley got

---

[42] Similarly, in Scotland during the Fifties and Sixties, when BBC Scotland broadcast a regular Saturday programme of Scottish dance music, people danced. Saturday being the day we visited our grandparents, there was the added bonus of having cousins arrive. Our mother and grandmother would make sure that the evening meal ('tea') was over, and the dishes done, so we would clear back the kitchen table and chairs ready for Jimmy Shand and his Band.

[43] Herbert Halpert, 'Preface' in Michael Taft, *A Regional Discography of Newfoundland and Labrador, 1904–1972*, p. iv.

their songs out to the neighbours. And if they were going to write a song about one another, or about what happens in the Valley, it was Jerome Downey whom they would seek out to sing them.[44]

Paul E. Hall (1897–1973)

Though I could not claim to know any of the song-makers well, I did visit Paulie Hall after hearing an anecdote in a kitchen ceilidh one winter's evening. A group of friends were reminiscing about mummering[45] and the fun they had going from house to house, 'sometimes miles in the snow'. Then, during the years when their children were young, it had been their turn to stay home and guess the names of the mummers. As one story championed another, one of the men turned to his wife with, "Remember that time the mummers came here and said that every year they came to our house there was a new baby crib? Anyway," he continued, as he told his story:

> These mummers stomped around and we were trying to guess who they were. And there was one of them went over to the crib to see our new baby and then turned around and said to everyone, "Oh, my word! Don't he look just the image of Paulie Hall?"

Only a couple devoted to each other might risk such a story, which evoked an uproarious response of both laughter and indignation. After it subsided, the husband smiled wryly, admitting he "Didn't think it was too darned funny at the time." His wife agreed, adding, "And I didn't like that either. Can you imagine? Paulie Hall!"

As the only one in the company who had never met the key character, I asked where he lived – perhaps I should visit him? Quick as a flash came the response, "Now's your chance! He might ask you to marry him!" And so, the following summer I returned to the Valley (wearing a shiny wedding ring) and soon arranged a visit to Paul's accompanied by thirteen year-old Karen Cormier and one of her school friends, a neighbor of Paul's. An excerpt from fieldwork notes written after the visit will set the scene:

July 15, 1970, Millville. Visit to Paul E. Hall

His house is situated on a hill c. 500 yards from the road; there's a trail cut through the woods to a cleared area of land. His small

---

[44] DVD 2007.

[45] Dressing in disguise, known as 'guising' in Scotland. See Herbert Halpert and George Story, *Christmas Mummering in Newfoundland*: See also, *The Last Stronghold*, pp. 107–117.

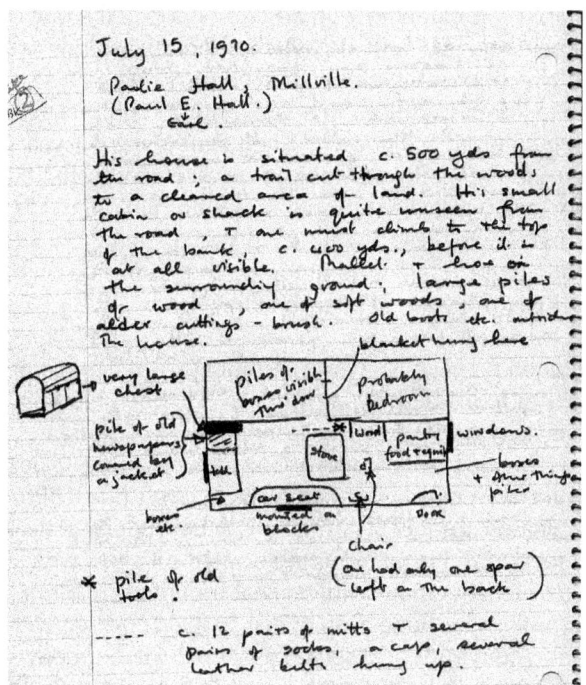

Fieldwork notebook, July 15, 1970 (Margaret Bennett Archive).

cabin or shack is quite unseen from the road and we had to climb to the top of a steep bank before it became visible. A mallet & hoe lie on the surrounding ground; large piles of wood, one of soft woods, one of alder cuttings – brush. Old boots etc. lie outside the house.

Above the stove, c. 12 pairs of mitts and several pairs of socks, a cap, several leather belts are hanging on a rail. In the main area, the kitchen-sitting room, the walls are covered with calendars from many years (1930s, 40s) to the current year, 1970. Many holy pictures and a 'Diploma' c. 24 x 18 ins. modeled on Papal Blessing documents. A diploma of "Spiritual Condition" given by the Bros. of Mt. Royal, as thanks for donations over a period of c. 12 years. (Name, Paul E. Hall inscribed on it.) On the same wall is a picture of a priest, Br. Andrew of Mt. Royal, said to have worked miraculous cures. Beside that is a postcard of Pope John whom he insisted was Bishop O'Reilly... Beside that, a calendar with a picture of the Queen in her coronation robes (1953). In the corner is a Sacred Heart surrounded by other calendars & pictures, mostly holy.

The table was cluttered with articles on top of the oilcloth. Old newspapers showed underneath the oilcloth, yellow with age. He had two photos which he showed us – one of his sister and her two children from 30 years ago, and one of himself taken at a logging camp at Millertown, when Paulie was 17 years old. A picture of Joey Smallwood took pride of place on the table. He was very proud to have shaken hands with him once. He 'spoke' to Joey [while we were there] – recorded on tape.

The family name 'Hall' is common on the north side of the Great Codroy River; they are of English extraction.

Though Paul cited his own his name as Paul Edward (Paul E. or Paulie) the Parish Records note his baptism as follows: 'October 17, 1897 I baptized at Grand River <u>Edward Paul</u> son of Joseph Hall and Margaret Gale, born October 1, 1897. Sponsors Isadore Gale and Matilda Gale'. On some occasions Paul also seems have cited his year of birth as 1896.

Paul was pleased to accept a neatly covered paper plate, 'Mom sent some supper for you…' He sat by his table and the visitors were comfortably seated, two on his 'couch' (an old car-seat mounted on birch 'junks') and one on his 'arm-chair' (a huge heap of newspapers covered with old jacket) between a box and a trunk that served as 'arms'. Had nobody spoken, this was a special visit not to be forgotten, for even the light in Paul's house was a unique experience – his windows were ingeniously 'glazed' with several thicknesses of re-cycled translucent fertilizer bags, which cast interesting shadows even before he lit his lamp. Paul did not mind the intrusion of the battery-powered reel-to-reel tape recorder with its cables and microphone, and seemed at ease being recorded as he talked about his life farming, logging and song-making.[46] This excerpt of verbatim transcription[47] gives the flavour:

Paul E. Hall: I made quite a few songs.
MB: How did you make them, when did you make them?
Paul: Oh, when I go haulin' wood, I had a little black mare, a beautiful little beast, and I didn't have to tell her what to do, she well knew, and I sat on me load o' wood up on top o' the hill and I could make up a song any day at all… I had a good memory; I'd come out in the night and scribbled it down, and den I'd get someone to either write it or type it. The most o' them was typed.
MB: Have you got any now [typed scripts]?
Paul: No, I give it to Charlie Samms, he wanted to write it and I give 'm the one was typed. 'The Bachelor's Lament'.

---

[46] Archive accession, MUNFLA C871-71-48.

[47] With thanks to transcriber Joan Kearley, Folklore Department, Memorial University of Newfoundland. Words in square brackets added for clarity.

MB: Do you still know it to sing?
Paul: No, dat was 26 verses.... I forgot them, I haven't sung a song for [a long time]. In fact, I never could sing. But I just done it for amusement in the backwoods, you know. It made a lot of amusement in the backwoods... when there was no radios or gramophones or anything then for entertainment....
MB: About how many did you write?
Paul: I made twelve or fifteen. I'm sure o' that many. Some o' them was long... Oh, I think I made twenty. Some o' them was short. And I'd start it, and a few words for a starting point, I didn't have to think over it at all, I could go on to get the air, an air that would suit it. I could go on and make the song and sing it, all at the one time. That was the hardest job to get the air for it. And then I'd start and just sing the song, and I didn't have to write it because I'd remember it... Betty Young, she used to, she wrote a good many o' them [down] for me and got them typed.
MB: She lived near here?
Paul: Yes, she lived there where Mike March is. She was Betty Corneilly, by the way.[48] She was Mr Corneilly's daughter... she couldn't sing nothing [of my songs] but she was a real – she was a good entertainer. She could sing, play the organ.
MB: What were the songs about?
Paul: Oh, I made different ones about the young fellers courtin', you know, teasin' them. Them would be shorter songs... I think I'm soon going to make some now about the young ones courting.[49]

In the wide world of song composition, today's song-makers talk of sitting down with a guitar or by the piano, with pen, pencil or computer keyboard, jotting down the song as it comes to them.[50] Paul belonged to an entirely different world of composing that had more in common with the old Gaelic bards, such as Duncan Bàn MacIntyre (1724–1812), for

---

[48] The Corneilly (or Cornelly) home was not far from Paul's family, and Elizabeth (b. 1901) was a contemporary of his. (She died in Halifax in 2004).

[49] Of the three songs in this collection, two of them are about courtship and both are aimed to tease the young people involved.

[50] Singer-songwriter Allan Taylor has produced a fine analysis of the techniques employed by modern song-writers in his Ph.D. study, *Song, Song-writing and the Songwriter in the English Folk Song Revival*, University of Belfast, 1993. Aside from analyzing his own techniques of composing, Taylor interviewed other song-makers including Tom Paxton, Ralph McTell, Leon Rosselson, Pete Morton and Wolf Biermann (from East Germany). The work is particularly important as it is presented from the point of view of the song-makers themselves, rather than ethnomusicologists outside their craft. See also, http://www.allantaylor.com.

whom Allan MacArthur had great admiration.[51] The Glen Orchy bard could neither read nor write, yet would return from a day on the hill reciting hundreds of lines that had come to him while stalking deer or carrying it home on his pony.[52] To Paul, there was nothing unusual about being able to retain lines of text without the aid of a pen, though he was pleased to have his songs written out at the end of the day.

Tunes seemed more of a challenge, as Paul explained to John Szwed that he had to work harder on getting 'an air that would suit' his songs. In his essay, 'Paul E. Hall: A Newfoundland Song-Maker and his Community of Song', Szwed states that "most of Hall's songs have melodies drawn from traditional folksongs and older popular ditties".[53] It may be, however, that Paul's expression 'getting an air' implies that he composed the tunes. Despite a long search assisted by other singers, I cannot identify any traditional tunes that match the songs in this collection, though one line in his song 'Micky Jim MacNeil' is reminiscent of 'I Met Her in the Garden Where the Praties Grow'.[54] By way of contrast, it is not difficult to recognise traditional tunes and melodic motifs in songs composed by the other two song-makers.

Micky Jim MacNeil (1901–1948)

The youngest son of James MacNeil (b. Codroy Valley, 1848) and his wife Jessie (b. Cape Breton, 1853), Micky Jim was born in 1901. Baptised Michael James MacNeil, he was known locally as Micky Jim, Micky or Mike. The family was among the first of the Gaelic homesteaders granted land on the south side of the Grand Codroy River in the settlement now known as Upper Ferry. Within two miles of the MacNeils' farm, all the families were Gaelic-speaking except the Martins, who were French, and although the children were all schooled in English, none could speak it before they went to school.

To recognise how strong the Gaelic language was in the Codroy Valley, it is worth making a 'virtual visit' along the stretch of road where Micky

---

[51] Allan had a remarkable knowledge of Gaelic bards and could not only quote some of their poems and songs but tell of their lives. See, *Dileab Ailean: The Legacy of Allan MacArthur*, 2010.

[52] Towards the end of his life, MacIntyre, who had become well known as a nature poet and song-maker, recited his compositions to the Rev. Donald MacNicol, parish minister of Lismore, who wrote them down. Running to thousands of lines, the poems with translations run to over 500 pages. It the style of oral composition that is being compared here, and not the content. See, Angus MacLeod, Editor, *Orain Dhonnchaidh Bhàin: The Songs of Duncan Ban Macintyre*, 1952.

[53] *Folksongs and Their Makers*, p. 155.

[54] One of the songs, 'The Bachelor's Lament', sounds rather like a piano exercise for the right hand, yet for the song it works well.

Jim MacNeil's people lived. Following the footsteps of the census-taker of 1921, when Micky was twenty, and 'knocking' only on ten doors[55], we find neighbouring houses occupied by the following families:

- Mr & Mrs John MacEwan (b. 1956 & 1861)
- Mr & Mrs Farquhar MacLellan (b. 1847 & 1859) and 2 sons (b. 1891 & 1896)
- Mrs Margaret MacArthur (widow, b. 1870)
- Allan MacArthur (widower, b. 1884), his widowed mother Jessie (b. 1849)[56], sister Sarah (b. 1892), brother Lochlin (b. 1896) and Allan's children (Lewis b. 1914, James, b. 1915, Frank, b. 1918 and Loretta, b. 1920)
- Mr & Mrs Dan MacNeil (b. 1869 & 1877) & 6 children (b. 1902 to 1912)
- Mr & Mrs James MacNeil, (b. 1848 & Jessie, b. 1853), son Hugh & wife Mary (b. 1891 &1890), John (b. 1888), Maggie (b. 1900) and Michael J. (b. 1901)
- M. & Mme. Charles Martin (b. 1861 & 1868) & 5 children (b. 1897 to 1909)
- Mr & Mrs Archie MacIsaac, (b. 1864 & 1871), daughter (b. 1905), nephew (1912), widowed aunt Flora Campbell, (b. 1849).
- Mr & Mrs Andrew MacIsaac, (b. 1879 & 1870) & 4 children (b. 1914 to 1919)
- Mr & Mrs Angus MacNeil (b. 1881 & Kate 1881), John MacNeil (widowed father, b. Cape Breton 1839), brother Thomas (b. 1891) and children Wallace (b. 1911), Bernard (b. 1912), Rita (b. 191), Gertrude (b. 1816), Winnie (b. 1918), Andrew (b. 1920).

Today, only the elderly folk in the Valley have memories of Micky Jim MacNeil, as he contracted tuberculosis and died in November 1948. At the mention of his name, 92 year-old Mary MacIsaac lit up with a bright smile: "Micky Jim? Oh, God, yes, I remember Micky" she laughed, "and was he ever funny! He could take off [mimic] anybody and make songs. Oh he was funny! And he lived down on this side of the MacArthurs' there. There was Hughie and Micky and Maggie – Hughie was married but his wife died at childbirth..."[57]

Neither Micky or his sister Maggie ever married, and their sister Cecelia, who had married Allan MacArthur when she was just seventeen, sadly

---

[55] *Newfoundland Census*, 1921. The ten houses are numbered in the records from 96 to 105. Only the families mentioned here, or elsewhere in the book are cited in full.

[56] According to Allan, his mother's name was 'Jenny'. She was born in Scotland (Moidart), and was a very young child when her parents emigrated.

[57] Fieldwork recording, June 28, 2012.

died a few months after giving birth to their fourth child. As can be seen from the 1921 Census (above), Allan was a widower with four children, the youngest only a year old.[58] He later re-married and the children from his second marriage got to know Micky Jim as "Uncle Mike – a gentle, quiet, witty man who worked in the Co-op Store." For several years, the store was the hub of the community, and when Margaret MacArthur (Cormier) left school at the age of fifteen, she worked there when "Uncle Mike was the manager. Oh, he used to be so good to us all, such a nice, nice man, and he was so funny."

When they grew up, the boys in the family referred to him as Micky, as Margaret's brothers Sears and Martin continued:

> He was related to Dad's first wife, and oh, a nice man. And it was Micky's father, Jim MacNeil, that cleared the land beside Dad in the early years, right from the shore [of the Grand Codroy River] to the base line, same as Dad.... He was a quiet man. He used to drink a glass of home-brew just once in a while, but not that much. And he wasn't loud or anything – oh no! He could recite – and he was good at it. And he made songs, like 'The Five Boss Highway' – Jerome sings it, but I never heard Micky sing the songs himself... he gave them out... But he got sick... and he died fairly young with TB, in St. John's, I think... They took him home in a box, to Doyles Station... I remember his brother Hughie meeting the train... Oh it was sad, because Micky wasn't very old... Just forty-seven. [59]

Yet, as long as the songs are sung, the voice of the bard is heard. In the context of his songs, Micky Jim MacNeil's 'voice' is particularly interesting as a reflection of his culture rather than of the personality known to those who lived and worked with him. Witty and funny, without a doubt, but gentle and quiet could not describe his bardic style, which had a fearlessness that bordered on risk-taking recklessness, as well as an edge that also characterized the compositions of his fellow song-makers.

Hughie O'Quinn (1905–1986)

Within the Codroy Valley and wider district of St. George's, it is well known that most folk who go by the name of O'Quinn are of French origin. (So ends the temptation to joke about these three song-makers as an Englishman, a Scotchman and an Irishman.) As any of O'Quinns in

---

[58] Further biographic details of the family, see, *The Last Stronghold*, pp. 62–67.

[59] Sears, Martin and Margaret were recorded June 26, 2012. The transcription combines their joint contribution. Their mother, Mary MacArthur, kept a journal in which she recorded the date of Micky's death as November 21, 1948.

the Valley will explain, priests from a bygone day, such as Monseigneur Sears (an Irish Gaelic speaker who learned Scottish Gaelic), had the habit of 'Hibernicizing' local names to fit with ones they knew from 'the Old Country'. Thus, when the priest was writing up the Parish Records after he baptized, married and buried them, Au Coin became O'Quinn, LeBlanc became White, Deveaux became Devoe, Benoit became Bennett, and so on. For a few years, families who went by these names managed to keep their own pronunciation only until their children went to school – when the teacher 'corrected' them.

Such are the ways of cultural assimilation and yet, Hughie, whose mother tongue was English, had a song-making style more associated with the Newfoundland-Irish than with the Franco-Terre Neuviens. He was also very much at home with the Codroy Valley Gaels, whose culture resonated with that of the Irish, especially when it came to house-visits (céilidh to the Scots and cèili to the Irish) as well as their inclination to song-making (particularly satire). Until the coming of electricity in 1962, the main entertainment was usually only as far as the next house, or along the road: wherever the gathering happened to be at the end of the day's work. Between Hughie's home and the crossroads at Doyles there were over a hundred MacIsaacs, all Gaelic-speaking, when Hughie was a boy.

Born Searston in 1906, Hughie was the fourth child of Joseph and Anna O'Quinn (b. 1859 and 1867), who farmed near the mouth of the Great Codroy River in the area known as 'the Block'. After attending the small, local school, where he was noted to be a bright student, he went to Ireland to enter the Seminary. In his day it was common – and in some families expected – to have one child who would enter the priesthood or the convent. After six years, however, Hughie had decided that the priesthood was not his calling, so he returned to everyday life in the Valley.

The time spent in Ireland undoubtedly made a lasting impression on Hughie's life. Though I have heard no account of exactly when Hughie went there, or why he returned home, yet looking at the Census Records before and after his sojourn, it is clear that there were major changes within the O'Quinn family: In 1921, when he was fifteen, he was one of six children living with both parents. (The following year, his 26 year-old sister Mary died of tuberculosis, which seems to have been rife at the time.) In 1935, however, only two people were recorded as living in the family home: Hughie, age 29, head of the household' and his father, age 78. It is possible that family circumstances may have affected Hughie's decision to return before ordination. Nevertheless, the years spent in Ireland were to influence him for the rest of his life, as can be sensed in his style of song-making.

For a few years he taught school in Millville, then, in the early 1940s Hughie 'did a spell' as manager of the Co-op Store, while continuing to farm at 'the Block'. He is widely remembered in the Valley as a likeable character, more than a little unconventional, 'great company', bright, witty, funny and slightly eccentric. Given his enjoyment of literature, particularly poetry and song, as well as his interest in history and traditional culture, he was drawn to the company of the likes of Allan MacArthur who lived along the road in Upper Ferry. Dan MacArthur, Allan's son, who was born in 1934, had vivid memories of their friendship:

> Oh, I remember Hughie! His sister married Duncan MacIsaac… And Hughie used to visit Dad's – I was pretty young, still at school. And one time I remember Dad and Frank [who was in his late teens] went down to Hughie's to get some hay – down to the Block, to Hughie's farm – and it was getting dark and they hadn't come back as they were still talking, and no word of the hay!
>
> And when he took over the Co-op store as manager, he had an old Jeep and he could never get it going [laughs] and he was supposed to be at work at 9 o'clock and probably it'd be 10:30, 11 o'clock and then we'd hear putt-putt-putt, this old Jeep'd go by the house [laughs] and that'd be Hughie!
>
> Anyway, finally he got a truck that was more up to date… and he wasn't used to driving in towns, and he went to Cornerbrook when the Highway went through. And he went up the wrong way of a one-way street and a policeman stopped him and he said, "Hey, Mister, this is one-way!"
>
> And Hughie said, "That's right, Officer, it's just one way. I'm going back home to Codroy Valley and there's just the one way". [laughs]

Though I met Hughie at various times in Dan's parent's kitchen, these were not the sorts of get-togethers where a visitor would be introduced as a song-maker, singer, musician or dancer, no matter how gifted they might be. Among friends and neighbours gathering for the 'craic' and the company, such attributes would only become evident as and when a suitable moment might arise. And, as in Ireland and Scotland, to introduce oneself in terms of any of these talents would be out of the question. As it is the character of the individual that matters most to the community, that is the main aspect portrayed and emphasised when memories are evoked. Biographical details become incidental, such as the fact that Hughie married was widowed and had one son who left home young[60] – "I think he went to work somewhere across, maybe Halifax…"

In the absence of immediate family members, the closeness of the community is evidenced by the interaction of neighbours, friends and more distant relatives, such as Loyola O'Quinn (1922–1995) who lived close-by. His children, who grew up in the sixties and seventies, looked on

---

[60] The family appears in the 1945 *Newfoundland Census*, St George's District: Hughie age 40, his wife Mary R. age 41 and son Kenneth J. age 3.

Hughie as belonging to their grandfather's generation. Lydwena (O'Quinn) MacArthur remembers Hughie as part of their large, extended family:

> We were all French one time... and [when I was young] Hughie was an old man – I think my father might have been his third of fourth cousin and we used to call him 'Mr Hughie'. He lived near us in a house by himself, but his house seemed really, really dark... My father fished with Hughie O'Quinn for years and years and years, and he used to come to our house for Christmas for dinner and every Sunday for dinner. And he played crib with Hughie – every night they had a game of cribbage and this time, Hughie counted his cribbage and he had none. And he said, 'Lolly,' – his name was Loyola – 'if I had a Mother Superior I'd start my own convent!' He had a way with words and he was very, very funny.
>
> And then Hughie won the Lottery one time! He won 25 thousand dollars on the Lottery, and when they asked him where he was going on vacation he told them Cape Ray! Can you imagine? Half way between here and Port aux Basques! They used to fish down at French Cove... Hughie liked to fish...
>
> He was so good to kids – years back he used to work at my Dad's store and he was very good to us children – he just loved us all. He used to play poker with us on Sunday afternoons then he wouldn't take any money. [laughs] And I remember one time when we were 'trick or treating' at Hallowe'en, and this time ... he had no candy left so he gave us a fruit-cake and a half a pie. A big one, for about six of us, and a half a pie!

In recalling how surprised and amused the children were by Hughie's unconventional offering, Lydwena raises three interesting points. Firstly, the visit to his house, which Lydwena recounts with warmth and affection, remains one of the family's most memorable Hallowe'en visits. Secondly, for Hughie's generation, the main time to go mummering was during the Twelve Days of Christmas, and in those days home-made fruit cakes were always regarded as a special treat – more than one slice would have been regarded as extremely generous.[61] And finally, as the term 'trick or treat' only gained currency after Confederation, Hughie was more familiar with the ways of Ireland and Scotland where, even into the 1970s, nobody had ever seen commercial Hallowe'en candy or heard the phrase 'trick or treat'.

Adapting to changes can take time, as I clearly recall from my first experience of a Canadian Hallowe'en in John's, October 1967. Though I had anticipated 'mummers' (known as 'guisers' in Scotland), when I opened the door I had no idea what the children were saying. 'Trick

---

[61] Mrs Mary MacArthur described how the women would begin in October to make fruit cakes for the Twelve Days. See, *The Last Stronghold*, p. 102.

or treat!' they chorused, adding a new phrase to my new vocabulary. So unfamiliar was the term that I could scarcely imagine it might eventually be adopted in Scotland. By the end of the twentieth century, however, both Scotland and Ireland had become so influenced by consumerism that even the fun of creating a 'get up' for Hallowe'en has been taken over by store-bought costumes. Had Hughie only taken a trip to Ireland to experience the impact of the Celtic Tiger and the arrival of American super-stores, no doubt he could have satirized in song the money-making racket that replaced the tradition he knew and loved.

Things may have changed in the Valley, but Hughie is well remembered, particularly 'down at the Block' where he lived. Neighboring farmer Joe Bruce, who was 'just a youngster when Hughie was up in years,' recalled:

> We referred to him as 'Uncle Hughie' even if there was no family connection. He was, of course, connected to relatives of ours, because he was married to Rita, who was related to Duncan Jim MacIsaac – he's in the song, 'When Duncan Jim that day fell in.' And I knew Hughie as a songwriter, because practically all the songs that he wrote I would know the background of it. Like, his 'Sealing Song' – you knew all the characters in the 'play' if you will... How did the boys feel about being immortalized in song? Probably happy about it, and realizing that 'It's my turn today and the next song will be about someone else – like John T. in his song 'The Roving Peddler'. In that one he was picking on John T. O'Quinn; he was the one that was growing the vegetables. And John T. would have been one of our class, because I was a farmer also.

Like Joe and his four brothers, John T. also liked to sing, and in 1959 was recorded by Kenneth Peacock for his National Museum of Canada Collection, *Songs of the Newfoundland Outports*.[62] The song he sang was not, however one of Hughie's, but a song he learned while working in a lumber camp, 'The River Driver's Lament'. With its "eat when I'm hungry and drink when I'm dry" chorus, it travels well and melodically it fits both the old-style unaccompanied singing as well as newer arrangements.[63] Yet such a song tells little or nothing of the community, except that the song was known and sung. Despite the fact that Peacock recorded several singers from the Codroy Valley (including Allan MacArthur and Lucy Cormier), he did not, however, include the text of any local songs from the area.[64]

---

[62] See, Vol. 3, pp. 759–760.

[63] The song has become widely known as the Newfoundland folk-rock band, 'Great Big Sea' have adopted it as part of their repertoire. They also acknowledge John T. O'Quinn of Searston as a source singer.

[64] He recorded Allan MacArthur singing one of his brother Murdoch's compositions, 'Oran an Tombaca' but only published the tune, without words, and made no

Peacock did, however, include some Newfoundland ballads or 'Come-All-Ye' songs, unlike song collector Maud Karpeles who made it clear that she wished to record 'old songs'. (Her main interest was in versions of ballads collected in England by her mentor, Cecil Sharp, of which there is only one in this collection.) After her visits of 1929 and 1930, she noted that some singers sang other genres that were 'a waste of time' and was dismissive of, if not irritated by, local compositions:

> I have tracked down a singer with a reputation for old songs only to be regaled with 'When You and I were Young Maggie' or 'The Letter Edged in Black'… songs are constantly being made up about contemporary events such as exploits at sea, shipwrecks, etc. They are often set to well-known 'Come-all-ye' type of tune. They usually have but little aesthetic value, and since my interest lay in songs that represent an older tradition I did not note any of them.[65]

As a result, there is no representation in the well-known Karpeles collection of song-makers such as Hall, MacNeil and O'Quinn, whose songs played a role in recording local incidents and aspects of their community, which may otherwise have been forgotten. At a time when the world of folksong scholarship seemed set to retain its focus on collecting 'classic ballads', American folklorist Herbert Halpert, who had spent his war years at the US Army base in Newfoundland,[66] was invited to present a paper to the 1950 International Folk Music Council in London. Halpert, who had an unforgettable style of oration and effective delivery, told his prestigious audience (which included Maud Karpeles) that:

> … the local song is much more significant for understanding the function of folk song in a community than is an infrequently sung or little known older ballad, no matter how much more satisfying the rare ballad may be to our aesthetic sensibilities, or our egos…. If singers do not make up new songs or manipulate the old materials, we have one indication that the singing tradition in that area has become fossilized.[67]

---

mention of the composer. See, Peacock, *Op cit,* p. 790.

[65] See Maud Karpeles, *Folk Songs from Newfoundland,* p. 18.

[66] While at the Harmon Base in Stephenville (less than 100 miles north of the Codroy Valley) Lt. H. Halpert collected stories and songs from the local people: "It saved my sanity during my army years." See, *Folklore: An Emerging Discipline: Selected Essays of Herbert Halpert,* p. 18.

[67] Herbert Halpert, 'Vitality of Tradition and Local Songs' pp. 35-40 (*JIFMC* 1951) p. 40. The article was later published in *Folklore: An Emerging Discipline,* pp. 135–142.

SONG-MAKERS IN TRADITION AND TRANSITION

In recognising Newfoundland tradition to be among the most vibrant that he had ever encountered, Herbert Halpert saw the urgency of recording it as widely as possible. And so, in 1962 he and his wife Violetta (also a noted folklorist) moved to Newfoundland, where he took up a professorship in the Department of English.[68] The position that was to be a step towards his main aim, and in 1968 he founded the Folklore Department that was to amass one of the largest collections of British Isles tradition in the world.

Sixty years after Halpert's provocative address to the International Folk Music Council,[69] there nothing fossilized about song-making traditions in Newfoundland. Several singer-song-writers have become well known outside of Canada, as have numerous bands and groups with a genuine Newfoundland stamp on their music.[70] Among them, a significant number acknowledge the Folklore Department at Memorial University as influencing their chosen path.[71]

In his valedictory address, at the end of a career dedicated to training students how to document and conserve traditional folk culture, Halpert stressed the importance of recording the context of song-making and singing. "In doing this," he explained, "the folklorist frequently finds he is collecting the oral history of a community." He continued with cautionary words of advice:

> I should stress to you, however, that folklorists are quite aware that a culture is never static but always changing. But for the folklorist

---

[68] See http://www.library.mun.ca/qeii/cns/special/Halpert.php

[69] Co-founder of the International Folk Music Council, Maud Karpeles, would not have agreed or even liked what he had to say. Notwithstanding, in 1970, in recognition of her work as an international ballad scholar, Halpert proposed her for an Honorary Doctorate at Memorial University of Newfoundland. When she returned to Newfoundland at the age of 84, Halpert took her on a fieldtrip to the communities she knew, accompanied by doctoral student Carole Henderson who recorded the trip: "She simply was not interested in the indigenous traditions... nor did she care to hear such songs when she returned..." See Carole Henderson Carpenter, 'Forty Years Later: Maud Karpeles in Newfoundland' p. 117, in *Folklore Studies in Honour of Herbert Halpert*, pp. 111–124.

[70] Best known is Ron Hynes, whose song 'Sony's Dream' has been covered by artists that include Dolores Keane, Emmylou Harris, Mary Black, Hamish Imlach, Phil Coulter and Rolf Harris. Professor of Folklore and Music at MUN as well as singer-songwriter and musician, Peter Narvaez discussed the song-maker as well as the world-wide impact of the song in his article, 'Sony's Dream: Popularity and Regional Vernacular Anthems' in *Sony's Dream: Newfoundland Folklore and Popular Culture*, pp. 154– 71.

[71] To mention a few, Denis Ryan of 'Ryan's Fancy', Anita Best and Jim Payne.

to study changes in culture, he needs to have a full knowledge of the past to serve as a base-line against which to monitor such changes.

In travelling to Newfoundland to undertake research, John Szwed acknowledged his indebtedness to Herbert Halpert's article of 1951, which first drew his attention to the importance of local song-makers.[72] In his essay in *Folksongs and their Makers* (1970) Szwed concluded that: "It is not an accident that song makers such as Paul Hall have disappeared at the time when mass media have made their inroads into the life of all the peoples of the world..."[73] While it very doubtful that a song maker "such as Paul Hall" could be found anywhere, it may be emphasised that it is not that song-making has disappeared, for it is very much alive in Newfoundland. Rather, it is that the style of composition is continually in transition, reflecting, as it does, the song-makers' thoughts, as well as the society in which they live and work.

While recognizing the impressive number of song makers in the Valley today – some only in their teens – Joe Bruce reflects on what has changed since Hughie O'Quinn's time:

> It's totally different today. There's no occasion to make a song [such as Hughie O'Quinn used to make, i.e. satire] and very little occasion to sing a song of that type. Because back then it was all house parties – visiting – and something would happen in the daytime and in the night at the usual gathering someone would put a little ditty to it, and put a few verses, then someone else picked it up and they'd add a few more. And it was something you'd just circulate around the community and very little of it was ever put on one of those things [recording machines].

Martin and Sears MacArthur also spoke of extemporaneous song-making among the Gaels, particularly when their father, Allan, got together with his brother Murdoch, a noted song-maker, who lived beside Hughie.[74] As children they were sometimes included, as the main idea was to have fun: "Remember that one, 'Oran nan Coin' [song about the dogs]?" laughed Sears, "and they'd be back and forth with a verse and making fun."[75] Then, when Martin began to sing a first verse, he looked to his brother for the second one:

---

[72] See, Szwed, *ibid,* end-note, p. 168.

[73] *Ibid*, p. 167.

[74] Best known of Murdoch MacArthur songs is 'Oran nam Mogaisean'. See, *Dileab Ailean*, pp. 66–70 and CD 2, tracks 15–17.

[75] Recorded June 26, 2012.

Dorobhan, dorobhan, thuirt an cù dubh
Tha mi gun bhrògan, thuirt an cù bàn –

The older generation in the Valley may seem to state the obvious when they remark that songs today are all made in English and nearly everyone sings 'with music' – accompanied by guitar, mandolin, button accordion or an entire band. Several have been recorded and are played on the radio – some "really good songs, but they're different," and, as Joe Bruce concluded, "Even my brother Ed, he made a few songs, but they're more 'Country' style."

Among local singers, the parallel or distinction appears in Jerome's family between two siblings born in two different decades: Jerome (b. 1923) represents the unaccompanied 'old style' and James (b. 1934), a singer-songwriter, the 'Country style' now more common all over Newfoundland. In the present day, children of the 'now generation' make an impressive contribution to social gatherings, whether in various kitchens or one of the community centres. From an early age they sing with ease and confidence, and are accustomed to adding in the jack-plugs of new technology, when there happens to be an amplifier in the corner of a kitchen.

At one such gathering in 2012, I asked one of Allan MacArthur's great-grandchildren to "Tell me about your songs, about the style you sing." Laying down her Dad's guitar, fifteen year-old Brittany Cormier explained that, "They're mostly 'Country' style, sometimes a touch of 'Pop'..."[76] There is a wealth of talent with no shortage of uncles, aunts, cousins to join in with the young, as (on that occasion) Brittany and her singer-songwriter cousin Mallory blended into the kitchen 'times' as easily as their parents and grandparents did. There seemed no need to ask how the young regard the older style of unaccompanied singing, as, when that 'turn' came around, their attentive listening (and joining in) demonstrated appreciation.

Yet it is not in the music that we meet the fundamental difference between 'then' and 'now', as the topics and texts of different generations of song-makers show. Ranging across personal relationships and affairs of the heart, to nostalgia for home, family or the old ways, today's multi-faceted songs appeal to the emotions without offending the sensibility of listeners. The same could not be said of the old-style song-makers represented here by Paulie Hall, Micky Jim MacNeil or Hughie O'Quinn, as all of them were capable of composing lines which, at the time, must have seemed very close to the bone.

---

[76] Recorded, June 27, 2012.

Following the Line of Tradition

While some may attribute the contrast in textual style to the current prevalence of political correctness, this may only be a small factor in accounting for the avoidance of any expression that could possibly cause offence. Yet, considering the personal memories of the three local song-makers represented in Jerome's singing – witty, warm-hearted, companionable friends and neighbours – it may seem curious, or even paradoxical, that in the role of 'village bard' they were capable of penning a song that all but crossed the boundary between embarrassment and libel. Nevertheless, song-making can only be understood in the context of the culture of those who compose songs, for, as Herbert Halpert emphasized, we need to have "a full knowledge of the past to serve as a base-line against which to monitor such changes."

Historically, the bard has had an honorable position in society, exemplified in Ireland and Scotland by the bardic lineage of centuries. As well as commanding respect, bards exercised social control to the point that people feared lest any indiscretion be publicly revealed in song. The tradition continued in the New World, where, for example in Maine, the woodsman song-maker Larry Gorman, whose songs continued to have a powerful effect on employers and workers even after he was gone.[77] Nobody was safe from the bard, not even other bards who, on one occasion might be delighted and amused by a fellow wordsmith, then, without warning, they may be tested and tried by the same one. (Such were the dynamics between Paulie Hall and Micky Jim MacNeil.) Even clan chiefs were wary of the bards, especially since many believed that they could become ill as the result of a satire.[78] Psychologically induced illness is nothing new; and, in truth, anyone might feel sick if they were scandalized in their own community.

As far back as 1695, when one of the earliest descriptions of Gaelic tradition was recorded in print, Martin Martin from the Isle of Skye (writing in English) noted in that the Gaels have a "gift of poesy" and an ability "to form a satire".[79] Nearly a century later, the Rev. John Lane Buchanan, a Gaelic-speaking minister whose parish was in the Outer Hebrides observed that, "One may meet, not only with studied, but even extemporaneous effusions of the most acute and pointed satire, that pierce to the heart, and

---

[77] Edward D. Ives produced a classic account on Gorman's life and songs in his book, *Larry Gorman: The Man Who Made the Songs*, (1964).

[78] It is well known among Scottish Gaels that some 'victims' were said to have broken out in boils after they had become the subject of a satire. Thomas A. McKean discusses the subject in, 'Tradition and Modernity: Gaelic Bards in the Twentieth Century' in *The Edinburgh History of Scottish Literature*, (2006) pp. 130–141.

[79] Martin Martin, *A Description of the Western Isles of Scotland circa 1695*, p. 13.

leave a poignant sting."[80]

The real sting or "bite" in the satire does not come from a wishy-washy portrayal of the subject, but from the dramatic or sharpened emphasis of key issues. This may be somewhat akin to caricature, where certain features are singled out by the artist and exaggerated, sometimes outrageously, with the aim of shocking observers into paying attention, so the satire can also take the listener aback. Scottish folklorist Alan Bruford described satire as the "stock-in-trade of most local bards ... and satire without truth or clarity cannot bite... they show much more of society than the eulogies of earlier bards."[81]

It is in the context of this tradition that MacNeil should be viewed, as he is a product of his own people. To the uninitiated, his compositions may seem hard-hitting, yet, compared to the effusive outpourings of some of older Gaelic bards, he is relatively mild and considerably kinder. His generation seems to mark a transition between satirists unafraid to reflect what others might only say behind closed doors, and song-makers whose livelihood could depend on the words they write.

That is not to say that, in general, current Newfoundland song-makers do not tackle contentious issues, for there is still a thriving song-making tradition, regularly provoked by political issues and government legislation affecting fishing and seal-hunting. Perhaps no single concern has been so forcibly expressed in song as the 1992 cod moratorium, which effectively put 30,000 Newfoundlanders on the dole. Expressions of anger and outrage abound, though they are directed *outside* of the local community, rather than *inside*, such as Eddie Coffey's naming of:

> The Portuguese, the Japanese, the Norwegians, and the French,
> And all the Spanish trawlers fishing there upon the Banks.[82]

Of course, even if the issue or incident that sparks off a song is resolved, that does not mean that the matter will rest or die. The song will keep it alive, as folksingers on both sides of the Atlantic show, for example, when they still sing compositions by the legendary Brendan Behan (born the same year as Jerome). Some can be heard to introduce a song of this genre

---

[80] John Lane Buchanan, *Travels in the Western Hebrides: from 1782–1790*, p. 80.

[81] Alan Bruford, Review of Ian Grimble's *The World of Rob Donn*. See *Tocher*, No. 35, p. 351.

[82] Peter Narvaez discusses over 30 Newfoundland song-makers who responded to the moratorium: '"She's Gone Boys": Vernacular Song Responses to the Atlantic Fisheries Crisis' (1997). Though the Codroy Valley is not represented in this discussion, there are still voices of dissent, as in 2012 Brendan MacArthur (Allan's grandson) penned a poem on the twentieth anniversary of the moratorium.

with a Behan quote such as: "It's not that the Irish are cynical. It's rather that they have a wonderful lack of respect for everything and everybody."

In the politically correct twenty first century, satirical song-making is alive and well, as Fintan Vallely demonstrates in his collection, *Sing Up! Irish Comic Songs & Satires for Every Occasion*.[83] A master at the craft himself, Vallely appropriately introduces the book as a "Gather-up of intolerance, irreverence, slagging and sedition" inspired by an experiment in 1987 "on the natives of Scotland [when he and Tim Lloyd performed a concert] of send-ups and other ephemera." Topics covered include those touched on, or tackled by, Paulie Hall, Micky Jim MacNeil and Hughie O'Quinn – for example, politics, courtship, employment, pretentiousness, animal rights, hypocrisy – with the culture of the day underlying the themes. There are also similarities in the style of composition (particularly in those by O'Quinn and MacNeil), as Valleley notes that "the verses are in the mould [sic] of both the 19th century seditions ballad and the music-hall skit. Moral judgment masquerades as wit in the best tradition of lightening the load."[84]

Humour is a curious thing, for, unlike other universally experienced qualities such as happiness or sadness, what passes for humour in one place may not be recognized in another. The Scots are fond of contrasting Glasgow and Edinburgh humour. A mere forty miles lie between the cities, but folk will tell you there is a million miles of difference between their sense of humour. In general, however, the Irish and the Scots share an ability to laugh at themselves, particularly through hard times. If there happens to be a shortage of hard times, we'll find something else to laugh at, if only the repetition of the worst things other folk say about us. We share a favourite in Samuel Johnson, for example, pretending to humble ourselves, in mock-reverence citing 'the famous Doctor Johnson'. Touch a nerve of national pride ("You actually *eat* oatmeal?), and out comes the definition: "A grain, which in England is generally given to horses, but in Scotland supports the people". Then (with no pause) the retort: "But where will you see such horses and such men?" The Irish, meanwhile, (if only to observe how you react) will refer to 'the Doctor' in quoting, "The Irish are a fair people. They never speak well of one another."

Banter peppered with 'one-liners', back-handed compliments and humorous insults are as common in the Valley as in Glasgow or Dublin. Visitors should arrive prepared for a taste, such as that which recently met me in Deer Lake airport: "Great to see you, girl!" says Jerome's former neighbour, Brian Farrell. He lifts my very heavy bag, suddenly scowling at

---

[83] Despite the title, the collection (2008) includes a few Scottish compositions by Glasgow's Adam McNaughtan and Ullapool's Andy Mitchell.

[84] *Sing Up!* Preface, p. 9. Though tempted to change this to 'mold', it remains as printed, since I was among the 'natives' at that concert when Fintan makes no bones about dusting off the mould of the past.

me, "My good God, Margaret! Whatcha you got in here? Home-baking?" His dead-pan expression gives nothing away while his wife shares my helpless laughter. "Brian can get away with that," Karen tells me, as we set off for 'home'.

GETTING CLOSE TO THE EDGE

What song-makers 'can get away with' largely depends upon how the audience relates to the subject and the opinions expressed. If, as in MacNeil's 'Five Boss Highway', the audience happens to *be* the subject, the song-maker may find there is a price to pay – in this case, the boss refused to give him a job. While there may seem little to lose in 'dashing off a song' about a controversial subject, it is quite another matter to release it. From that point on, the potential impact seems to call for a risk assessment in terms of how it might affect the song-maker as well as the subject. Yet, nobody, apart from the song-makers themselves, would be able to tell if such issues concerned them. Judging from their output, however, and the fact that they gave their songs to Jerome to sing, there is no implication of regret.

If there is any regret regarding the song-makers represented here, it is only that I was too late to ask them about how they dealt with public opinion. Nevertheless, as these same questions are still relevant today, song-makers who have taken such risks are in the ideal position to answer. As far as satirical song composition is concerned, in Scotland there may be no singer-songwriter better qualified to speak than Dick Gaughan, whose international acclaim does not conceal his reputation for ruffling feathers wherever he sings.[85] And, as someone who can now look back on more than forty years of song-making, he is in a position to know if the passage of time dims the youthful passion for addressing issues of incompetence, injustice, racism, social liberty or any of the others he has tackled. On reflection, his answer is clearly 'No':

> I spent my life getting up people's noses, and some of it's deliberate. Sometimes I consciously attempt to disturb people. If you're going to make any kind of contribution as any kind of artist at all you have to be prepared to be a grain of sand in people's shoes and make the comfortable a wee bit less comfortable, and the smug a wee bit less smug. [laughs] Sometimes you have to do that, you know! Like, 'I'm gonnae offend you, you bastard, because I want you to think about this, I want you to understand why –'

---

[85] As the question arose during an informal discussion between participants at 'The Gille Mòr Festival' in Thurso, March 2012, Dick agreed to be recorded for this project. With us were poet George Gunn and songwriter Nancy Nicolson who could also relate to Dick's views. See also: http://www.dickgaughan.co.uk/.

If you write, you're going to put somebody's nose out of joint – I don't care, which is probably why I'm poor! [laughs]

Singers who 'cover' Gaughan's songs will no doubt to do so for years to come. Yet, it is not to perpetuate his name that he composes, but to keep alive a public conscience, world-wide or local. It is in their songs that such song-makers reveal unique characters unafraid to stand by their convictions. And as long as there is one singer, such as Jerome, to keep the songs alive, then their songs will live on.

ATLANTIC GUARDIAN
THE MAGAZINE OF NEWFOUNDLAND

IN THIS ISSUE:

THREE PICTURE STORIES

LEWISPORTE TO FOGO
A VISIT TO "TWIN TOWNS"
VETS' BALL IN BROOKLYN

FEB. 1949
20c
Vol. VI, No. 2

ATLANTIC GUARDIAN VISITS the twin towns of
CHANNEL and PORT AUX BASQUES

● THE NAMES of the "twin towns" of Channel and Port aux Basques remind us of those days in the history of Newfoundland when there were no Newfoundlanders but only fishermen from England and the coasts of Europe. Basques from the French and Spanish Pyrenees fished the gulf and the waters of the south-west corner of the island. Channel Islanders or Jerseymen were to be found here and there from Southern Labrador around the west and south coasts to Conception Bay. The people of the "twin towns" today are neither Basques nor Channel Islanders but 3,000 sturdy Newfoundlanders. There are not even any descendants of the former, for the Basques never settled here and had ceased to fish these waters long before anyone thought of settling in Port aux Basques. The mere fact of the existence of the town of Channel is a tribute to the courage and hardihood of its inhabitants for the little soil left there after the glacial period has long since been eroded, due chiefly to the lack of vegetation. Its raison d'etre was of course codfish and the area is well known for its winter fishing.

(Continued on next page)

The coming of the Railway made Port aux Basques the main gateway between Newfoundland and Canada. The fine new ship, the S.S. Cabot Strait, makes in about eight hours the crossing between North Sydney, N. S. and Port aux Basques, over the waters after which the ship is named. For many years this run was made by the S.S. Caribou, until she was sunk by a German torpedo during a crossing on the night of Oct. 14th, 1942. Among the 133 who lost their lives were Captain Tavenor and his two officer sons, natives of Channel. A monument has been erected at Port aux Basques to the memory of those who went down with the Caribou.

Since their incorporation in 1945, the towns have made giant strides in civic improvement. The terrain is most difficult for roadmaking yet already one mile of modern road has been built with their own machinery at a cost of $42,000.00. Town lighting was effected in May, 1947, at a cost of $3,700.00, the power being

bought from the West Coast Light & Power Company at Grand Bay.

Cattle control regulations have made it possible for people to plant trees, lawns and flower gardens. Some have brought soil twenty miles for this purpose.

Modern fire fighting equipment, including a pumper fitted with wheels in summer and skis in winter, has been purchased and already proved itself a sound investment. Wells have been protected, building regulations instituted, sanitation improved tremenduously and a Town Inspector appointed.

The council members at present are, reading from left to right: Samuel Walters, Eric Huelin, George Norman (Chairman), Fred Murrin (Clerk), Norris Cousins. Members not shown in picture are: Garfield Walters, (Vice-Chairman), I. E. Davis (Secretary), William Lawrence, Joseph Feltham.

There is a Council Office building and a shed for housing the road machinery and fire fighting apparatus. The town war memorial can be seen near the Public Building pictured on the opposite page. The Caribou Monument is shown here.

THE SONGS & A STORY

Labrador Rose

I ventured to walk early one summer morning,
With the dew on the ground and the sun shining clear;
I spied a wild rose growing there on the mountain,
My heart skipped a beat o'er the vision I seen.

In the vision I saw the face of my darling,
Its petals her hair, its perfume her smile;
The stem of the rose was her body so slender,
As it reached out for life from the rich mountain soil.

Oh, Labrador Rose, you're the rarest of flowers,
As you blossom and grow by the cold northern stream;
For the rest of my life I will stay here beside you,
Oh, Labrador Rose, you are one living dream.

Each morning I walk in the dew in the sunshine,
To be with my flower as it grows on the moor;
There's nothing around to compare with her beauty,
Oh, flower, so rare, you'll be mine evermore.

Oh, Labrador Rose, you're the rarest of flowers,
As you blossom and grow by the cold northern stream;
For the rest of my life I will stay here beside you,
Oh, Labrador Rose, you are one living dream.

Composed by Dick Gardiner of Labrador City, 'Labrador Rose' was one of the one of the songs that Jerome also liked to play on accordion. If he and Rosie happened to be at a kitchen party, folk would soon be on the floor waltzing and singing the refrain. As both Jerome and Rosie loved to waltz, he'd smile with pleasure as he sang. Then, as is the way at those kitchen 'times', no sooner would Jerome lay down his accordion than another player would take over for the next waltz – their waltz.

Over the years, 'Labrador Rose' has become part of the dance band repertoire in the Newfoundland; yet every time I heard Jerome sing it, I sensed it had a special significance to him. Though I didn't ask him (somehow it seemed too personal), eventually I asked his grand-daughter, Dale, if she thought that this was Jerome's special song for Rosie. Without hesitation she replied, 'Oh definitely, no doubt about it!'

The Badger Drive

There is one class of men in our country,
That never is mentioned in song;
Now, since their trade is advancing,
They'll come out on top before long.
They say that our sailors have dangers,
And likewise our warriors bold;
But there's none know the life of a driver,
What he suffers with hardship and cold.

With their pike poles and peaveys and bateaux and all,
They're sure to drive out in the spring – that's the time;
With the caulks in their boots as they get on the logs,
It's hard to get over their time.

Billy Dorothey he is the manager,
And he's a fine man at the trade;
When he's around seeking drivers,
He's like a train going down grade.
But still he's a man that's kindhearted,
On his word you can always depend;
And there's never a man that worked with him,
But would like to go with him again.

With their pike poles and peaveys and bateaux and all…

The drive it is just below Badger,
And everything is working grand;
With a jolly good crew of picked drivers,
 And Ronald Kelly in command.
 For Ronald is boss on the river,
 And many jobs more you may know;
 He drove the wood off the Victoria,
 Now he's out on the main river drive.

With their pike poles and peaveys and bateaux and all…

I tell you, today home in London,
The Times it is read by each man;
But little they think of the fellows,
Who drove the wood on Mary Ann.
For paper is made out of pulpwood,
And many things more, you may know,
And long may our men live for to drive it,
Upon Paymeoch and Tomjoe.[1]

With their pike poles and peaveys and bateaux and all...

So now to conclude and to finish,
I hope that ye all will agree;
In wishing success to all Badger,
And the A.N.D. Company.
And long may they live for to flourish,
And continue to chop, drive and roll;
And long may the business be managed,
By Mr. Dorothey and Mr. Cole.

There can be few Newfoundlanders, if any, who don't identify with the 'Badger Drive' or join in the chorus, not only because of its popularity as a song, but also because of its relevance to every household. Learning to handle a saw and an axe is part of every boy's upbringing – in times past it was more important than formal schooling, as every house, church and school was heated by wood and every building and outbuilding dependent on the skill of the woodsman. Moreover, there was the pulp and paper industry with its endless demand for timber: another world compared to that of the woodsmen who worked from home. For young men, the prospect of earning a wage and the possibility of adventure was what lured them to work in a lumber-camp (regardless of the conditions) for it was often the only way to make a living.

Small wonder the song became a favourite at 'kitchen times' all over Newfoundland, where it is generally taken for granted that the words of the chorus are as well known as the standard equipment of the loggers. For the uninitiated, however, a brief summary of the logging tools may be useful, as times have changed in today's mechanized lumberwoods: 'Pike poles' are long poles (12 to 10 feet long), with a sharp spike on the end, used for controlling the logs while floating them on a river. Peavey hooks or 'peaveys' (usually spelled 'peavies' though it is named after the inventor, Peavey), are shorter wooden-handled tools (usually 3 to 4 feet 6)

---

[1] Tributaries of the Exploits River.

with a spike that is rammed into the log to 'grab' it, and a hooked 'arm' to engage the log so that the driver can have leverage to roll, pull or float the log into position. The bateau is a shallow, flat-bottomed boat, easy to maneuver, and developed to withstand dangerous river conditions. The raft that transports the supplies for the river was sometimes called the 'Mary Ann'. And, as the drivers had to balance on floating logs and often leap from one log to another, the soles of their calf-length 'caulked' ('calked' or 'corked') boots had to have numerous sharp spikes to prevent them from sliding off into the water. The loggers and river-drivers soon learned the 'lingo' of this dangerous work, with phrases in everyday speech, such as 'look out for the widow makers!'

Life at the logging camps was only for the strong and the fit, and those unconcerned with home comforts. Every winter hundreds of men from all over the island would head for the lumber-camps in Central Newfoundland. Despite the distance of over 250 miles, many went from the Codroy Valley, including Paul E. Hall who told me he first went there at the age of seventeen (1913). Over the years, whatever hardships he experienced seemed to fade into insignificance. Another old woodsman in Quebec told me that some nights you'd bunk down in your boots – you might never get them back on your feet if they froze overnight[2]. Yet life in the lumber-camp is best remembered for the camaraderie, the yarns and the songs that Paulie enjoyed during of "the shortest winter I ever put in".[3]

In Upper Ferry, Paulie's contemporary Lucy Cormier (1898–1983) also recalled her brothers bringing home new songs they learned in the lumbercamps, such as 'The Banks of Sweet Dundee', 'The Little Mohee' and 'The Lady LeRoy'. She sang them until well into her eighties, as well as the French songs that were already part of her repertoire: "Well I learned these songs from my brothers – they used to go in the woods, you know, and when they came home they had songs and that's where I learned them. That was the year I was married (1918) and that's not yesterday..."[4] And, as can be seen from the prolific song collecting of Canadian folklorist Edith Fowke (as well as others), singing played an important part in lumbercamp life.[5] Edward D. Ives, who interviewed several woodsmen, also recorded

---

[2] See, 'Lumbering' in M. Bennett, *Oatmeal and the Catechism*, pp. 80–88.

[3] Paulie's account paints a much more appealing picture than some recorded from lumbermen twenty years later when men spoke of nights spent in the freezing woods because they couldn't reach camp, dilapidated bunkhouses that were full of lice, and the boring diet of beans. See Dufferin Sutherland, 'The Men Went to Work by the Stars and Returned by Them: The Experience of Work in the Newfoundland Woods during the 1930s'.

[4] The recordings I made of Lucy in 1970 are accessioned MUNFLA 71-048 C888 to C892, and songs co-recorded with Kenny are MUNFLA 80-134 C4791.

[5] A selection of her recordings of woodsmen can be heard on "Lumbering Songs from the Ontario Shanties" (Folkways FM 4052), Smithsonian Center for Folklife and Cultural Heritage, 1961.

descriptions of their particular enjoyment of Saturday nights singing song after song till late in the night, as Sunday was their day of rest.[6]

At work, however, danger was never far from the loggers and was the constant companion of the men who hired on for the drive – one slip and you're gone, drowned or crushed to death by the logs. As former lumberjack Robert E. Pike put it: "Working from unstable bateaux or on treacherous jams, the riverman had to be as agile as a panther and surefooted as a mountain goat merely to survive."[7] These were the men celebrated by John V. Devine when he composed his song, 'The Badger Drive' in 1912. According to local and family tradition, "Devine composed it in a Grand Falls boarding house after having been fired from his job as scaler for the Anglo Newfoundland Development Company (A.N.D.) [Then] he sang the song at a St. Patrick's Day concert at which company officials were present and allegedly won his job back."[8] The setting is the logging town of Badger, 20 miles west of Grand Falls, which is the biggest paper mill-town in Central Newfoundland.

Situated beside the fast-flowing Exploits River, (the longest river in Newfoundland), the mill-town was set up in 1909 by the Anglo Newfoundland Development Company (A.N.D.) and supplied with timber by satellite logging towns such as Badger and Millertown (20 miles west of Badger).[9] Granted, the paper and pulp industry in Newfoundland has generated employment for over a century, but the greatest benefits may have been to the newspaper industry in Britain, where (as the song says), readers of *The Times* spare not a thought for the hardships or dangers producing that paper.

The song is a perpetual reminder of the realities that are important to singers such as Jerome, who keep these issues alive through their singing.[10] Jerome was also a skilled woodsman, though happily he worked from

---

[6] See, Ives, *Joe Scott: The Woodsman Songmaker*, pp. 371–402.

[7] Robert E. Pike, 'Log Drive on the Connecticut', p. 30.

[8] For a fuller discussion on the song, see John Ashton, '"Badger Drive": Song, Historicity and Occupational Stereotyping' in *Western Folklore,* Vol. 53, No. 3 (Jul., 1994), pp. 211–228.

[9] The planned town of Millertown was created by Scottish timber baron Lewis Miller from Crieff. See, http://www.communityofmillertown.ca/index.php

[10] The song has many commercially recorded versions, the best known being by John White, star of Newfoundland's long-running and most popular TV show, 'All Around the Circle'. See also, www.youtube.com/watch?v=PORqrPq5nro combining John White's singing with remarkable archive film footage of the dangerous logging operation. White does not, however, sing the verse Jerome sings about readers of *The Times* in London. The song is in many printed collections, including the complimentary booklet (Bennett Brewing Co), *Songs Of Newfoundland*, pp. 28–29. See also, Greenleaf and Mansfield, *Ballads and Sea Songs of Newfoundland*, p. 324. Roud Folksong Index 4542.

home with his horse and sleigh: "I spent a lot of time in the woods. I used to cut all kinds of wood and haul it and sell it – that's how I kept myself alive!" (2007) Along every road in the Valley, neatly stacked cords of wood accumulated over a winter's work tell the same story for dozens of households: it's a way of life which, as long health endures, can go on well into old age.

After he had 'done his stint' in the lumbercamps as a teenager, Paulie settled back into a life of seasonal work of winter familiar throughout the Codroy Valley.

When asked about his time in the lumber-camp, however, Paulie remembered the very best of it, which, at the end of the day, is the wisest way of dealing with life's hardships:

Paulie: You worked till the stars was in the sky, from morning till night – you'd see the stars in the sky 'fore you'd come outa the woods. While you could see how to work you stayed in the woods – that was the rule. But after the 15th o' March you'd work from seven [in the morning] till six [at night].... You'd meet people from all over the country... And on Sunday we'd go from camp to camp – the camps would be about a mile apart, I imagine. And we used to visit one another in the camps... get acquainted with a lot of folk at the camps. Victoria River was only a narrow river, but a *big* river, and 'twas deep, but you could go to three or four [camps] on the opposite side, see, and three or four camps on our side. And the shortest winters that I ever put in. I was over eight months in there one year. I went in sometime in – I believe it was *nine* months. I went in in September and I landed home the 9th o' June. And you can imagine now the time, times like it was then – I come out, you'd get no money, draw no money till you come out to Millertown. I never drawed a cent till I come out!

MB: What was it like staying in the camps?

Paulie: Oh, it's lovely there, warm, and a great big giant stove about this long and so high, and you'd chuck in a junk o' wood the size o' this kettle, and with the coals [embers] that's there, there's fire all night and fire when you get out [of your bunk] in the morning.

MB: Who looked after the fire?

Paulie: Oh, the cook, he had to keep that fire on. There's a cook and a *cookie* in them places, and the *cookie* is the handyman – bring in the wood and do the outside work, carry water and so on, look after things and sweep out the bunkhouse every day. Oh we had it comfortable.

MB: And was the bunkhouse made of logs?

Paulie: Yes, and stogged it wi' moss. And then when the snow come, six, seven foot of snow in there, in the interior of the country, and shovel show up against it. And the top was covered with tarred papers[11].

MB: All winter long –

Paulie: I was paid enough; I had quite a bit o money and I went into the Royal Stores, that's the company store, to get a suit o' clothes and to fit meself out to come home. And everything was sky high. So I jumped on the A.N.D. train and come out to Millertown Junction and I went to a Jew by the name o' Boulos. I got a suit o' clothes, a cap, a shirt, a collar and tie, a pair o' boots – laced up boots – dress socks, cap, cost me a little bit over $11. Now today you wouldn't get the boots.

MB: My gosh! You'd hardly get the socks today!

Paulie: You wouldn't get them at all – they were all leather boots; the whole thing was leather. And a lot o' people'll say they're hard times. It was better times then than it is now... You just handles more money now and 'tis not as good to you. You don't get as good a material today as you'd git in them days.

MB: What did you do when you came home from the lumber camps?

Paulie: Oh I farmed and I was staying home then – that's where I was born to.

---

[11] 'Tar paper' as it is generally known, is made by impregnating heavy-duty paper with tar to produce a waterproof material useful for roof construction. Usually the roof is then tiled, though Paul's own house simply had a tar-paper roof.

The Anti-Confederation Song

I'm lonesome since in 'Thirty-two
we lost Dominion status,
No longer can I summon strength
to sing "O Fhir a' Bhàta".
A foreign gang came over here
to rule and gather taxes,
While natives toiled to till the soil,
or labour with pick-axes.
No fun or frolic do I crave,
my heart it is a-bleeding,
Since we our heritage have lost
and others us are leading.

Now, by the way, the experts say,
our country's self-supporting,
Joe Smallwood hopped the west-bound sleigh
the Maple leaf a-courting.
Oh shall wed the great Confed?
Or shall we court the Yankee?
Or shall we bide at Mama's side
and use the self-same hankie?

I mind the time while in my prime
I tried my hand at batching.
Why should I wed a battleaxe
to guide my course of action?
If history's lessons we would learn,
a vassal's trade we'd shun, sir,
We'd man our vessel stem to stern
with native crew to run her.

Old Newfoundland was quite devoid
of any real devotion,

Until Confederation hit
the hearty Nova Scotian.
They moved o'er here from year to year,
with no thought of returning,
Till one contacted DDT
and it set his heart a-yearning.

His souvenir did disappear
and he was sorely tempted
To regain with speed the only breed
from Federal Tax exempted.
He sold his flock of purebred hens
to help defray expenses,
He must regain his bosom friends
before he'll lose his senses.

And now my news is running out,
and gee! I feel like dancing.
I hear Joe Smallwood's got the gout
and he must quit romancing!
So clear the floor and let her roar,
for joy that almost blinds me,
We'll sing and dance to the merry strains
of "The Girl I Left Behind Me"!

Jerome was of the generation of young men and women who were in the prime of life when Newfoundland joined confederation in 1949. They were the last generation to have been seen adulthood as 'Newfoundlanders born and bred', and the first of a generation to raise children who would be Canadians. To many couples (including Jerome and Rosie), there were children born on both sides of that divide, and, as I was to discover from fellow students when I first went to Newfoundland in the late 1960s, it was common to hear young folk say they were proud to be Newfoundlanders. Though they themselves could have no real memory of confederation, yet they proudly claimed their birth-right and wore it like a badge of honour. To their credit, many were knowledgeable about their history, not only as one of Britain's oldest colonies[1], but also about the circumstances that led to confederation with Canada.

---

[1] The history of the self-governing British colony, which became a British Dominion in 1905, is as complex as the pre-confederation debates. One of the options considered was that Newfoundland might join the United States, hence the reference to 'court the Yankee'.

3. THE ANTI-CONFEDERATION SONG

There can be no doubt that political songs possess an enviable power to keep alive issues which may have first come to light through a newspaper headline, a radio broadcast or a fiery political speech. From newscast to newscast one crisis seems to fizzle out as soon as the next one emerges; but if it becomes the subject of a song, even small details may be remembered for years, even centuries. Sometimes when a political or social issue seems settled, the song about it may lie dormant until there is a resurgence of strong sentiment. Then suddenly an old song may be given a new lease of life.

Such was the case with a song composed in the lead up to the 1869 election, when Newfoundland voted not to join the Dominion of Canada – the 'Anti-Confederation Song' was penned by an unknown composer of that era: 'Come near at your peril, Canadian Wolf!' More than sixty years later it was 'collected' by Gerald S. Doyle [1892–1956], a devotee of Newfoundland traditional culture and folklore, who was an enthusiastic song collector, amateur film-maker as well as an astute businessman. In 1927 he had the vision to compile and publish a selection of songs in a booklet, which was distributed freely all over Newfoundland as a sales promotion for his patent medicines. So popular was this this promotional songster that he published four more, and, to this day, the impact of these five little books can still be heard among singers.[2] 'The Anti-Confederation Song' (collected by Doyle) was also available on 78 rpm records, thus broadcast on local radio stations, and though it was well known in the Valley, by the 1940s it was clearly out of date. And so local song-maker Hughie O'Quinn soon composed a new Anti-Confederation Song that addressed some of the issues of the day and also named the main political figure. Written from the point of view of folk living just 'across the Gulf' from Nova Scotia, and sung to the tune 'The Girl I Left Behind Me,' O'Quinn's song has a west-coast flavor. In line 2 he refers to one of the Gaelic songs popular at every ceilidh – *Fhir a Bhàta*[3] – and though not a Gaelic speaker himself, Hughie could join in the chorus, as could Jerome.

As with any lead-up to political change, by the late 1940s there was intense debate about the pros and cons of becoming Canada's tenth province. Most vocal among the pro-confederation campaigners was Joseph R. Smallwood (1900–1991), a charismatic character whose voice was already known on radio. His popular programme, 'The Barrelman', had

---

[2] Doyle also published a book, *Old-Time Songs And Poetry Of Newfoundland: Songs Of The People From The Days Of Our Forefathers*, which has 'The Anti-Confederation Song'; see p. 69.

[3] The song *'Fear a Bhàta'* was particularly popular at millings, which lasted in the Codroy Valley until the early 1960s. Allan MacArthur, who lived on the same side of the river as Hughie O'Quinn, often sang the verses while the entire company would join the chorus, beginning 'O fhir a bhàta' (See Peacock, p. 786). Frank MacArthur, Allan's son, also had a version, published in M. Bennett, *Dileab Ailean: The Legacy of Allan MacArthur*, pp. 31–32 and Track 7 of accompanying CD.

a strong content based on Newfoundland's rich cultural heritage.[4] A man of seemingly tireless energy, Smallwood's speeches and radio broadcasts highlighted the benefits of a better education system, health provision, the development of pulp and paper mills, iron ore mines, as well as hydro-electricity. 'Joey' as he was popularly called, became a household name, and though he was by far the leader in the race, neither the man himself nor the idea of confederation was everybody's choice. Nevertheless, he became the 'Father of Confederation', as he was lected the first Premier of Newfoundland and Labrador in 1949. He remained in office until 1972, when, after a dynamic career he enjoyed an active retirement into his nineties.

Thanks to Jerome's singing, however, Hughie O'Quinn's Anti-Confederation Song is still in circulation more than half a century after the political questions have been settled.

---

[4] See Peter Narvaez, 'Joseph R. Smallwood, The Barrelman: The Broadcaster as Folklorist' (1983) in *Canadian Folklore Canadien*, (1983), pp. 60–78. Smallwood also wrote his autobiography, *I Chose Canada: The Memoirs of the Honorable Joseph R. "Joey" Smallwood* (1973).

The Bachelor's Lament

There is a house upon a hill
That is a bachelor's hall
And the bachelor that lives in it
His name is Paulie Hall.

To my tippy-tippy-tippy tip-top, tip-top, tip-top
Tippy-tippy-tip-top tay.

Now as I may tell you
I'm living at my ease
I go out just when I'm ready,
I come in just when I please.

I do all my own cooking,
And I wash and mend my clothes.
Sure on every second Friday,
Why, I polish up my stove.

I do all my own outdoor work,
I milk and get my wood.
Sure I do it with a right good will
As a good old bachelor should.

I have no wife to bother me,
Or to spend on paint and rouge.
So you see I have some extra
When I want to have a booze.

Right now you may imagine
What she'd spend to buy a puff.
If you had it at The Island View[1],
'T would buy you beer enough.

---

[1] Paul wrote: 'If you had it in a beer shop' (Szwed, p. 158), and this is what Jerome would have heard originally, as the Island View Restaurant only opened in the late 1970s. At other times, Jerome sang the line as, 'If you had it in a billfold…'.

When a month's work it is ended
After a mighty hard drag,
I'll step out on some fine evening,
And take on a great bit jag.

Next morning when I get up
My head is mighty bad,
And I hear no woman scolding,
You bet I feel some glad!

Now if I had a woman,
You would hear her scolding 'damn!'
By the look upon her cross face
She was eating sour jam.

I wish I knew some nice young lass
To love and carry home
Sure I'm getting mighty tired
Of this living all alone.[2]

I'm going fifty-fifty,
And to you I'll tell no lies,
Now there's Margaret Bennett watching,
She's the devil for the boys![3]

Some fine spring in the June month
When my last seed it is sowed,
And there's not one tree left standing
On my farm below the road,

When all this work is ended
That I have planned in my mind,
I'll go searching through this wide world
Till a partner I will find.

I can't get a wife round here,
You all know how hard I looked,
So I'll join the train at Doyles,
And I'll go to Journois Brook.

And for a bait at Journois Brook
I'm gonna take a hen,

---

[2] Not in version noted by Szwed.

[3] Not in Szwed

Sure, and as soon as I arrive there,
'Tis courting I'll begin.

With a Rhode Island Red in under me coat,
Sure don't you wish me luck?
Sure, and in my britches pocket,
A stick of old Black Duck.[4]

And when I get at Journois Brook,
In order for to win,
I will give me coat a little shake
And out will pop me hen.

I'll stay around at Journois Brook
For one week and a day,
Sure, and if I haven't got one
Then I'll go on to Flat Bay.

I'll stay around at Flat Bay
Till all the girls are grown,
Then I'll tighten up me collar
And I'll go to Shallop Cove.

I'll stay around at Shallop Cove
Till "No," the girls all said,
And once more I'll cut me whiskers off
And try around Bank Head.

I won't stay long at Bank Head,
Me heart will be so sore
I will say, "To hell with the hen and girls,"
And go to the Labrador.

And every little Husky girl
That I see far or near
I will pop the question to her,
"Will you marry me, my dear?"

I've sung you all the latest songs,
The latest I have learned,
So I hope to hear another one,
Another in return.[5]

---

[4] Chewing tobacco. (The brand is also produced in flake or smoking tobacco).

[5] This verse may be Jerome's own composition, perhaps a word from the singer, as it doesn't appear in the one Paul gave to Szwed.

Songs about bachelorhood abound, each with its own take on the woes, disadvantages, frustrations, lamentations misadventures as well as advantages, delights and freedom of the unmarried man. Best known among singers may be the English folksong, 'The Foggy, Foggy Dew', popularised in the 1940s by Burl Ives and still well known on both sides of the Atlantic. There may be no song on the subject better known to Folklore students or scholars, however, than this one, as it was the subject of a widely read study by John Szwed:[6] 'Paul E. Hall: A Newfoundland Song-Maker and his Community of Song', one of three case studies that comprise the book *Folksongs and their Makers,* co-written with Henry Glassie and Edward (Sandy) Ives.[7] In his introduction, Ray B. Browne hailed the work as 'ground-breaking' and 'trail-blazing' as he concluded:

> ... in the thoroughness and newness of their approach and coverage, [these studies] bring new light to bear on the creative process, the sources and kinds of stimuli bearing on composition, the influence of the artists' background and foreground. They are, therefore, both exciting and informative in their own right and are landmarks in the study of the creative process and the creator.[8]

It is unlikely that Paul ever guessed how widely known his song or his name were to become when he invited the passing anthropologist into his home. Szwed's vivid description records the event: "Paulie stepped out from behind a bush... and began a conversation... it was as though he had been preparing for my visit for decades... In Paulie's house ... I heard an autobiography as carefully fashioned as a bard's epic."[9] It was on that visit that Szwed noted 20 verses of this song, which he discusses at length from the point of view of the anthropologist. He concludes his discussion suggesting that his "approach to understanding the song's meaning does

---

[6] In the mid 1960s, anthropologist and ethnomusicologist John F. Szwed was Research Fellow at the Institute of Social and Economic Research at Memorial University of Newfoundland. Better known for his biographic studies of Jelly Roll Morton, Miles Davis and Alan Lomax, Szwed is Professor *Emeritus* of Anthropology and African American Studies at Yale University, and currently Professor of Music and Jazz Studies at Columbia University. In the late sixties he became well known to Kenny Goldstein, as he joined the faculty of the University of Pennsylvania while Kenny directed the Folklore Department.

[7] For the benefit of those 'outside the field', Glassie and Ives are two of the great names in international Folklore studies. Individually, their published works in Ireland and Scotland have also made significant impact on trans-Atlantic scholarship. Szwed's study of Paul E. Hall is pp. 147–169 in *Folksongs and Their Makers* and since its publication, the book features on reading lists for students of folklore and ethnomusicology.

[8] *Folksongs and Their Makers,* p ix.

[9] *Ibid*, p. 152.

not exhaust the possibilities.... with its numerous allusions that beg for psychoanalytic interpretation."[10] Such analysis is outside of my field, as my folklore methodology is as 'participant observer' of general sharing of day-to-day life, which includes community events, family occasions and kitchen 'times' where music and songs are interspersed with anecdotes and jokes. Among the singers and listeners, however, I have not heard (or asked for) discussion or analysis on the 'hidden meaning' of a song described as 'just to tease' or just for fun. There is no doubt, however, that recording the song-maker on his own, as Szwed did, without an audience or a sense of 'performance' of the song, completely changes the dynamics between fieldworker and 'informant'.[11]

For Kenny, hearing Jerome sing 'The Bachelor's Lament' was one of the highlights of his visit, as he had not heard it sung before that.[12] Thirty years on, the recording of Jerome is singled out as one of the gems from two summers, and over seventy hours of tape, now archived in the Special Collections of the University of Pennsylvania Folklore and Ethnography Archives in the 'Kenneth S. Goldstein Recorded Sound and Manuscript Collection':

> This is one of our more extensive holdings, and to date only the collections made in the years 1978–1980 have been made fully accessible through cross-indexing... Many of the works are native to Newfoundland, and the songs of Frank MacArthur [son of Allan MacArthur] are of particular interest... Students interested in John Szwed's article on Paul E. Hall, in *Folksongs And Their Makers*, should note that 'The Bachelor's Lament' discussed there is recorded on tape T-80-00002-114. Jerome Downey sings this and other songs by Paul E. Hall, as well as songs by other local composers.[13]

---

[10] *Ibid*, pp. 157–162.

[11] Szwed's discussion with Paul on the places mentioned is particularly insightful in relation to that one-to-one interview.

[12] In an otherwise favourable review (*Folklore Forum*, 1972), folklorist Elliot Oring wrote, 'It is only unfortunate that the Popular Press did not issue a small companion disc recording of the songs.' (I have tried, so far without success, to ascertain if a recording exists.)

[13] See, Kenneth S. Goldstein Recorded Sound and Manuscript Collection, Special Collections, The University of Pennsylvania Folklore and Ethnography Archives, http://www.sas.upenn.edu/folklore/ [My square brackets] As the recordings are not (as yet) on line, the release of Jerome's recording may offer the first opportunity of hearing the actual song. While Szwed notes (p. 162) that 'the implications of the title are important,' in his article the song is discussed as 'The Bachelor's Song'.

During that memorable session, Jerome had already sung two other local songs when Kenny asked him if there were 'other song-makers around here':

Jerome: Paul Hall, well you'll know him?
MB: Yes
Jerome: Well, I try one of Paul's... [*he sings a shorter song, 'Mary Kate White'*]
KG: So Paul Hall wrote a lot of songs?
Jerome: Oh quite a lot. All local. Very local, though. He wrote one on himself, that's probably the best one he wrote.
KG: Sing that one.
Jerome: Well, it's long, it's awful long. I might break down and have to have a spell... Oh, well, this is 'The Bachelor's Lament' and it's by Paul Hall.

Then, tapping his foot to a steady beat, Jerome effortlessly sang twenty-three verses with expressive phrasing and remarkable breath control. (Listen for those verses sung in one breath.) His sense of enjoyment is evident, as his is engagement with the song, the audience and the song-maker. Though Paul Hall was, by then, no longer alive, Jerome seemed to reflect some of the sport they had once shared, adding to the fun by extemporaneously naming a young women in the company (Karen Farrell) just to catch her by surprise and tease her. So successful was he that, to record a track without extraneous exclamations, he had to sing it again. (His second 'take' was equally effective, as he changed the name yet again, though this time the laughter was stifled till the end of the song.) When the mirth subsided and Kenny asked about Paul, he too was taken by surprise, as Jerome segued from his response into an amusing story – a *true* story that began, 'I remember one time...' And so, having set the scene, it's over to the story on the next track.

Paul E. Hall Story

KG: When did Paul Hall live?
Jerome: Oh, I guess he was born around about 1896 and he died in 1972.
KG: Oh my gosh, that's a long time!
Jerome: laughs
KG: Did you learn that song from him?
Jerome: Yes. I learned it from Paul
KG: Did he write it out for you, or did he just sing it?
Jerome: No, he just sang it.
KG: Was he a good singer?
Jerome: Well, he wasn't too bad.
KG: Where did he live?
Jerome: Well, he lived in Millville, down the road from here about three and a half, four miles. I remember one time, he came up, he was down at the garage here, he was all dressed up, you know, like a guy that was going to New York or some place, and I said to him – because he was a guy just like myself, most of the time only dressed in rags.[1]
So I said, 'Paul, what in the name of God are you doing today, all dressed up like you are?'
Well, he looked at me like that for a while and then he said, 'I might as well.'
And he stopped, and I thought he was finished.
And then he said, "Everyone else is working."
And then he stopped another nice while, you know, and he said, "It's a poor town can't afford one sport!"

Laughter

---

[1] Jerome refers to the serviceable clothes worn during outdoor work, such as checked flannel shirts, overalls and heavy boots. By contrast, best clothes were for Sundays and special occasions.

In the world of folk-music, it is fairly common for singers and musicians to introduce songs and tunes by weaving in personal anecdotes into their performance set. Less common, however, is the ability to 'get it right' in terms of what teachers would call 'good stage craft'. Jerome had an enviable natural ability to put his listeners at ease and hold their total attention without ever seeming to seek it or draw attention to himself. As a result, he seemed to have a presence about him that eludes many who aspire to such. Newcomers to the stage (and even some of the 'old hands') might welcome Jerome's example in terms of what does, or does not, work as an engaging introduction.

In telling a story such as this, Jerome provides an invaluable role model to those seeking to improve their skills relating to this aspect of performance. Teachers, too, can welcome his example, as they know how difficult it is to teach this craft to musicians or singers who insist on telling personal experiences of no interest to their audience. (Given the choice between a short, witty anecdote such as this one, and a long, rambling account of a hang-over, the audience response shows that the first can be told again and again, while the second is best forgotten.)

Just as with singers who can hold an audience with every song, so with story-tellers, who have discovered that 'timing can be everything'. The story told here is 45 seconds long. Such is the skill of the true artist.

Pat Malone Forgot that He Was Dead

Things were dull in Irish town;
everything was going down,
And Pat Malone was getting stuck for cash.
In life insurance he had spent
all his money to a cent
And business with him was going smash.

His wife Bridget to him said,
"Pat, my dear, if you were dead,
All that hundred thousand dollars I would take."
So Pat lay down and tried
just to play off he had died
Until he smelled the whiskey at the wake.

Then Pat Malone forgot that he was dead.
And he sat up in coffin and he said,
 "If this wake goes on a minute,
sure's the Devil I'll be in it,
 So you'll have to make me drunk to keep me dead."

First they gave him a sup,
after that they filled him up
With old-time gin and laid him on the bed.
And before the break of day
everybody felt so gay
They had quite forgot poor Pat was lying dead.

Then they dragged him from his bunk,
still alive but awful drunk,
And laid him in his coffin with a prayer.
Then the cabman loud did shout
that he never would pull out
Until he saw somebody pay the fare.

Then Pat Malone forgot that he was dead,
And he sat up in coffin and he said,
"If you're here to doubt my credit,
you'll be sorry that you said it,
So pull out before the corpse will break your head."

Why, then they started out
on the cemetery route,
The mourners tried the widow to console.
Until they reached the base
of poor Pat's last resting place
And so gently there they lowered him in the hole.

Then Pat began to see,
just as plain as you or me,
That he'd quite forgot to reckon on the end.
When the sods began to drop
he burst off the coffin top
And so quickly to the surface did ascend.

But Pat Malone forgot that he was dead,
As out of the cemetery he quickly fled.
He nearly made a blunder,
'twas a lucky chance, by thunder,
That Pat Malone forgot that he was dead.

Spoken:
I guess Pat Malone forgot that he was dead, it's pretty evident!

Though this song stirs up stereotypical images of an Irish wake (with situational comedy in the presence of death), the 'dollars and cents' instantly evoke an Irish-American setting. The nineteenth century saw Irish people in their thousands emigrating to America, particularly during the Potato Famine (1946–51) and the impoverished aftermath. Most headed to New York or Boston where they could work, send money home, put up with the slum conditions and strive for a better way of life. For many, material possessions were almost non-existent, but the immigrants were rich in things that mattered: traditional skills, music, stories, songs and an irrepressible sense of humour, with thousands of kinsfolk to share it.

During those years, the rise of music-hall entertainment in the cities (noted for comic skits and songs), as well as vaudeville and Tin Pan Alley (from the1880s to the Depression of the 1930s), proved well suited to the wit of Irish song-makers and performers. As respite from a hard week's labour, people would flock to enjoy light-hearted entertainment, and, if they could afford it, might buy a gramophone record of a favourite song. Hundreds of music-hall songs were recorded on 78 rpm discs, usually sung to piano accompaniment, and once the records were released, the songs spread like wildfire. Then, as now, the music business cashed in on every show, with recording studios and sheet-music printers sending their mass-produced wares all over the world.[1]

'Pat Malone Forgot that he was Dead' can be dated to sheet music printed in 1895 by Petrie Music Company in New York, which credits Harrry C. Clide with the lyrics, James J. Sweeney with the melody and H. W. Petrie with the piano arrangement.[2] The song was first recorded in 1902 by one of America's most prolific recording artists of his time, New York vaudeville singer Dan W. Quinn, (1859–1938). Though he had over thirty 'hit records', the songs he recorded are now better remembered than he is: 'Daddy Wouldn't Buy Me a Bow-wow', 'The Band Played On' and 'Casey Would Waltz with the Strawberry Blonde'.[3] As the 'Pat Malone' record was released twenty years before radio broadcasting began in the North America, whatever popularity it enjoyed was not due to the 'wireless' as it was called.

When the folklorist-collector asks the singer, 'Where did you get that song?' and the answer is, 'Oh, I just heard it somewhere,' that can be accepted as the truth. Wherever he heard it, is now anybody's guess. Looking at the sheet music and listening to the old 78 record, however, we may be certain that neither one was Jerome's original source, as he was a stickler for words and 'the right tune'. Even though he did not read music, Jerome sang dozens of songs, hymns and sacred compositions such as 'Jerusalem' and 'Ave Maria', which ably demonstrated his accuracy in learning melody and words. Entertainment aside, Jerome's version of 'Pat Malone' raises (and proves) some very interesting points regarding song acquisition and performance. Even when a song has a clearly defined origin (sheet-music or gramophone record) it can still enter oral tradition and find its way to firesides, lumbercamps, church socials and village halls thousands of miles from the platform that launched it.

Along this path, some songs take on variants such as one might expect to come across in ancient ballads or broadsides. In a folk-song collecting project set up by the Wisconsin Historical Society in the late Thirties, for example, there is another version of 'Pat Malone Forgot that he Was Dead'.[4] Though the song

---

[1] A catalogue of sheet music from the 1830s to the 1930s indicates the level of business of New York printers alone, as it lists over 5,000 titles for Irish songs. All genres are included, from traditional Irish ballads to Irish-American music-hall compositions. The titles also give an interesting insight into what people were singing during those years.

[2] Thanks to the Lester S. Levy Collection of Sheet Music, Department of Rare Books and Manuscripts, Sheridan Libraries, The Johns Hopkins University, http://levysheetmusic.mse.jhu.edu See, Box 054, Item 098.

[3] Dan W. Quinn is commemorated in America's Songmakers' Hall of Fame.

[4] Recorded in 1941 from Robert Walker in Crandon, Wisconsin and archived by the Wisconsin Historical Society as DT #529, the song later appeared in a collection by Harry B. Peters, *Folk Songs Out of Wisconsin: An Illustrated Compendium of Words and Music*, (1977).

tells the same story as the original and evokes the same images, (justifying its claim to be the same song), yet, as with Jerome's version, the wording is not as written by the lyricist.[5] Melodies change too, a note here and there (possibly by accident), or an entirely different tune, such as the one Jerome sings. And, when it comes to performance, unlike Dan W. Quinn, who affects a 'stage Irish brogue', Jerome sings in his own voice, whether his audience be two or three folk by his own fireside or a packed house in the high school auditorium or community centre.

Having met in his travels too many singers with 'phony accents', Dominic Behan wrote 'A Note to Young Singers' urging them to "open your mouth, and, whatever your voice is like, sing!"[6] That said, it helps considerably to be blessed with a warm, melodious voice and the instinct to use it as Jerome did.

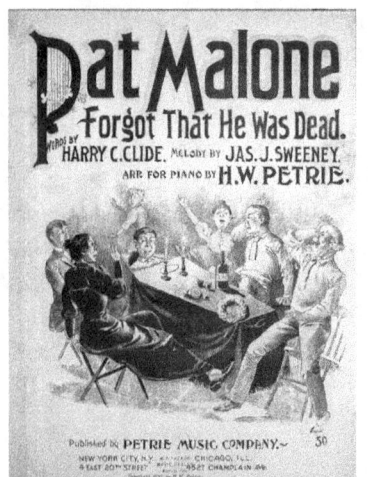

Courtesy of Lester S. Levy Collection of Sheet Music, Department of Rare Books and Manuscripts, Sheridan Libraries, The Johns Hopkins University, http://levysheetmusic.mse.jhu.edu.

---

[5] G. Malcolm Laws also includes it in his compendium, *American Balladry from the British Broadsides*, classified under 'Humorous and Miscellaneous Songs' (Section Q), in his sub-section, 'The Irish Wake', number Q18. This classification suggests it to be an original *broadside*, however, rather than printed sheet-music recording the names of the composer, lyricist and arranger.

[6] From the liner notes to the American edition of Dominic Behan's L.P. 'Finnegan's Wake', reprinted as an introduction to his book *Ireland Sings*, (London, 1965), p. 2. While Behan gives sound advice, it would be difficult to agree with his explanation that academics, song collectors and educators are to blame for young singers using a phony or stage accent. Jerome enjoyed singing at least one of Behan's own songs, 'Liverpool Lou', which he also played as a waltz on accordion.

The Road to Dundee

Cauld winter was howlin' o'er muir and o'er mountain
And wild was the surge on the dark rolling sea,
As I met about daybreak a bonnie wee lassie,
Wha asked me the road and the miles tae Dundee.

Says I, "My wee lassie, I canna well tell ye
The road and the distance I canna well gie.
But if you'll permit me tae gang a wee bittie,
I'll show ye the road and the miles to Dundee".

At once she consented and held out her hand.
Not a word did I speak wha the lassie may be,
She seemed like an angel in feature and form,
As I walked by her side on the road to Dundee.

At length wi' the Howe o' St Martin[1] behind us,
And the spires o' the town in full view we could see,
She says, "Gentle Sir, I can ne'er forget ye,
For showing me so far on the road to Dundee".

This ring and this purse take to show I am grateful,
And some simple token in trust you'll give me.
Then bravely I kissed the sweet lips o' the lassie,
E'er I parted wi' her on the road to Dundee.

Well here's to the lassie, I ne'er can forget her,
And every young laddie wha's listening to me,
Ne'er be afraid to convey a young lassie,
Though it's only to show her the road to Dundee.

<u>Jerome was the first</u> person in Newfoundland (and in those days the *only*

[1] The Howe o Strathmartine

person) I ever heard sing 'The Road to Dundee'. Generally speaking, little seems to be known of the origin of this old favourite, though it has been popular in Britain for well over a century and appears in many song-books, on countless records and CDs, and can be heard at concerts and informal gatherings from Scotland's northernmost isles to the south of England.[2]

No matter how familiar or commonplace a song may be, however, enthusiastic collectors are always interested in gathering every version of it that can be heard or found.[3] That Jerome should sing this song for two 'collectors' – one of whom, Professor Kenneth S. Goldstein (known to everyone as Kenny) was an internationally known collector, folklorist and record-producer, and the other a young, newly graduated student of Folklore (MB) – seemed more than serendipitous, as it generated a story that merits re-telling. Jerome's rendition of 'The Road to Dundee' had an immediate connection to Kenny's seminal work in Scotland (1959–60), when, as a Fulbright scholar, he spent a year recording some of the country's finest ballad singers. Living (with his family) among the folk of the North-east, Kenny immersed himself in all aspects of oral tradition as well as every book, songster and manuscript he could find.

One of the most important collections he worked on were the files from a Scottish newspaper *The Buchan Observer,* which ran a newspaper feature called 'The Ballad Corner' encouraging readers to 'write in to the paper' with their own songs.[4] The column ran from 1907 to 1911 and was the joint project of schoolmaster Gavin Greig (1856–1914) and the Reverend James Duncan (1848–1917). They were members of a club, which held lectures

---

[2] A small booth in Dundee selling song-sheets and broadside ballads (The Poet's Box) printed a version probably based on a poem by Fife poet Charles Gray. (The first verse sets a bleak picture: 'Grim winter was howlin' owre muir and owre mountain/ And bleak blew the wind on the wild stormy sea/ The cauld frost had lock'd up each riv'let and fountain/ As I took the dreich road that leads north to Dundee.') The song, however, has a rather brighter story, which has appealed to singers and listeners for over a century. The song turns up in many collections, including the British Museum, where it catalogued in the Roud Folk Song Index, number 2300. See also John Ord, *Bothy Songs And Ballads,* p. 152 and Nigel Gaither, *Songs and Ballads of Dundee,* note 63, p. 132 and two versions with music, pp. 125–28. Roud 2300.

[3] As far back as 1800, Walter Scott (whose role models were Allan Ramsay and Robert Burns) wrote a note to fellow collectors James Hogg, William Laidlaw and John Leydon to write down even 'partially remembered fragments' of ballads while they helped him prepare for his *Minstrelsy of the Scottish Borders.* Further discussion, see Margaret Bennett, 'Living Tradition' in *Scottish Traditional Literatures* (forthcoming 2012).

[4] Newfoundlanders will be familiar with the same type of column in papers such as *The Family Herald.*

and discussions relating to the North-east[5] and, judging by the papers that survive, the area was well served by lively talks from the 'dominie' and the minister. The collection amassed over 3,000 contributions, and among them, four versions of 'The Road to Dundee'. The intention was to publish the entire collection; but, apart from an index and selected articles and papers, neither of the men lived to see the publication in its entirety. [6] It was not until Kenny spent a year in Scotland that the collection received long overdue attention when he collaborated with Greig's grandson, Arthur Argo, to reprint the publication that contained this very song.[7]

Twenty years on, Kenny's expression reflected his particular pleasure in hearing Jerome sing the familiar 'Road and the Miles to Dundee', with only one minor textual difference: In Jerome's last verse, when the girl gives her ring and purse and asks for 'some simple token' in return, she simply receives a kiss. In most of the Scottish versions, however, the love-token given is a gold pin, and *then* she receives a kiss:

> I took the gowd pin from the scarf in my bosom,
> And said, "Keep ye this in remembrance o me."
> Then bravely I kissed the sweet lips o' the lassie,
> Ere I parted wi' her on the road to Dundee.

Curiously, even in Greig's day, this same verse was already a matter for discussion, as can be seen from his note in the newspaper column: "I have made several records of this popular song. They correspond pretty closely until they come to deal with the parting of the somewhat strange couple." Such are the details that singers and collectors love to discuss as they continue to share the vibrancy of folksong.

---

[5] Originally known as the Spalding Club, (1839–1869) and later the New Spalding Club, (1886–1928), members gathering and conserved documents and manuscripts now archived at Aberdeen University. One of the aims was to hold lectures and discussions relating to the North-east and to publish proceedings. While most of the material was of historical or literary interest, there were several ballad enthusiasts, including Greig and Duncan.

[6] Gavin Greig also saw the publication of *Folk-Song of the North-East:* Articles Contributed to the 'Buchan Observer', 1909–14, but it was a very short print-run, which quickly went out of print. After both Greig and Duncan had died, editor Alexander Keith made a selection of the classic ballads from their collection and published *The Last Leaves of Traditional Ballad Airs*, with an introductory essay and notes (1925).

[7] Gavin Greig, *Folk-song in Buchan and Folk-song of the North-East*, Foreword by Kenneth S. Goldstein and Arthur Argo); see article 51. The entire collection was later published in 8 volumes, edited by Patrick Shuldam-Shaw, Emily Lyle and others. See *The Greig-Duncan Folk Song Collection*; 'The Road to Dundee' (song number 971) is in vol. 5, pp. 99–104.

John Park He Had Nar' One

We got six dollars and a half
When we landed at the wharf,
And when we carried them to the store
We got a dollar more, sir.

CHORUS, between every verse:
    Not much of a hand on board a vessel,
    On board a vessel, on board a vessel,
    Not much of a hand on board a vessel,
    A-fishing the puppy swile, sir.

We wrote a letter right away,
And posted it without delay,
We sent it down to Jamie Baird
For a couple of gallons of rum, sir.

Next Saturday morning as you might see,
Two gallons of rum did come to we,
We carried it down without being seen
So far as Georgie Wall's, sir.

The very same evening after tea,
A crowd of people came to we,
And an excellent time as you may see,
Till coming on the morning.

Just then a little disturbance arose
Everyone was getting his own,
For everybody had his girl,
While John Park he had nar' one.

Up steps Jack to Tom Patey,
"What you been doing along with she?"
She used to go along with me,
She will the same this morning."

Why, Jack and Tom got in a clinch,
And neither one was made to flinch,
And when the fight came to an end
The maiden she was gone, sir.

Come all young men take warning by this
And never go fighting over a lass,
For it will only cause a laugh,
And you'll be left with nar' one.

The song was also known in the Codroy Valley as 'Not Much of a Hand Aboard a Vessel'. Anticipating that the title may not be entirely understood by listeners from outside Newfoundland, Jerome began by telling an oft-told anecdote to demonstrate the usage of an old Newfoundland word, 'narn', meaning 'none'.[1] Often shortened to nar' (or extended to the phrase 'nary a one'), it may be best understood in context of this old chestnut:

> This fellow went fishing one day and when he came back, his friend wondered if he caught anything. So he asked him, 'Ar fish?'
> 'Nar' fish,' was the reply.
> That's 'Any fish? No fish!'

"And I learned the song from my father when I was about ten years old," he added. Although Jerome said no more about the setting, his brother Joe recalled that, "Dad used to sing, but not so much in the house – it would always be when he was working, usually outdoors. Jerome might have heard it too from old Tom Cornelly[2] – he used to go down to their house when he was courting Rosie."

In everyday speech in the Valley, a phrase such as 'A crowd of people came to we' would not generally be heard, even though the use of 'we' for 'us' is common in other parts of Newfoundland. Joe, who had heard variants of the song elsewhere, explained that the individuals named in the song were not from the Valley: "Jack Park and Georgie Wall were names from Cape Ray, and Jamie Baird was a merchant in St. John's[3] who would

---

[1] *The Dictionary of Newfoundland English* gives 'not a single one' as the meaning.

[2] In the MacEdward Leach Newfoundland Collection, 1951, there is a recording of Tom Cornelly, which is very close to this version, with the same grammatical usage and same tune. See, http://www.mun.ca/folklore/leach/sounds/NFLD2/23-07_51.mp3.

[3] Originally from Ayrshire in Scotland, the Baird firm became part of Newfoundland's social history. Besides supplying wines, spirits and groceries, they became involved in the cod and seal fisheries and also in politics. See Melvin Baker, 'Prominent Figures from our Recent Past: James Baird'.

supply rum." Then, on the subject of 'we' and 'she' the former schoolmaster took a moment to reflect on where he had first heard it. With his wry sense of humour, Joe recounted a classroom anecdote enough to make any teacher smile, as well as remember the pupil and the situation:

> Sixty years ago this form would be used in Cape Ray[4], Codroy[5] and other parts of Newfoundland, but not in the Valley. I remember teaching school in Parsons Pond[6] and asking a question from the catechism:
>
> Question: "Can God see us?"
> Answer: [from named pupil] "He can see we but we can't see he."

English language specialist and folklorist John D. A. Widdowson identifies phrases such as 'he don't know she' as originating in the south-west of England, particularly Cornwall, Devon, Dorset and Somerset. He explains that, 'the pronominal system in Newfoundland retains many archaic and dialectical features, notably in the West Country English speech type.'[7]

Of the song itself, the theme is one that could travel the world, from fishing port to fishing port: Landing the catch puts money in the pockets, then, from that point on it's an age-old story that could be told in many variants the world over. No matter how often an entire wage is squandered on alcohol, no matter how out of hand things get with drink, and no matter how often fights break out over women, it will all happen again regardless of the oft-repeated caution, "Come all young men take warning by this..." And, lest any of the crew be tempted to glorify the work that went into earning their money for booze, the chorus repeatedly reminds the hired 'hands' of their inadequate efforts.

---

[4] West of Port-aux-Basques, on the south coast of Newfoundland.

[5] This village is right on the sea-coast, beyond the area settled by the Scotch, the French and the Irish. Apart from language usage differences the religion is predominately Anglican, whereas most of the Valley is Roman Catholic. See, *The Last Stronghold*, p. 26.

[6] On the Northern Peninsula, in the district of Bonne Bay.

[7] In his Introduction to *Folktales of Newfoundland*, (co-authored with Herbert Halpert), John D. A. Widdowson discusses variants of language usage and syntax across the island. (See pp. lxxvi).

There's A Bridle Hanging On The Wall

There's a bridle hanging on the wall,
And the saddle in an empty stall.
There's a faded blanket in the hall,
And a bridle hanging on the wall.

With a pony for my friend I used to ride down the trail,
Watching the moon swing low.
Now that faithful friend has found the end of the trail.
He's gone where all the good ponies go.

And his bridle's hanging on the wall,
And the saddle in an empty stall.
No more he'll answer to my call;
And his bridle's hanging on the wall.

In days past, almost every household in the Valley kept a horse. It was essential for farm and woods work, as well as for local transport. Even into his eighties, when he had stopped full-time work, Jerome still had a horse for occasional work. No doubt there is a bond and affection between horses and their owners, but farmers and woodsmen are most unlikely to express it in sentimental words; it's just a matter of being good to your horse.

This cowboy 'weepie' was composed by Rex Allen, (1920–1999), the 'Arizona Cowboy'. A well-known singer-songwriter, and one time movie star in the popular Roy Rogers movies, Allen had several successful compositions, (including his million-selling single, 'Crying In The Chapel'). In 1936, 'There's a Bridle Hanging On the Wall' was recorded by Carson Robison and his Pioneers, and a few years later by Nova Scotia's Wilf Carter (1904–1996) who became known as the 'father of Canadian Country Music. As Jerome's brother Joe recalls, this was one of those songs on the radio that made its way into the family sing-arounds so warmly recalled by his generation.

Teaching McFadden to Waltz

Charlie McFadden he wanted to waltz,
But his feet weren't built that way,
He went to a professor and stated his case,
Said he was willing to pay.
The professor gazed down at his feet in alarm
As he viewed an enormous expanse
Then tacked on a crown to his regular price
For teaching McFadden to waltz.

Chorus:
One two three, balance like me
You aren't quite a fairy, you have your faults,
Your right leg is lazy, your left leg is crazy,
But don't be uneasy I'll teach you to waltz.

Well he finally got the tune into his head
But it wouldn't go down to his feet
He sang loving ditties from morn until night
Counted his steps in the street.
One night as he went to his bed to retire
After painting the streets bright red
He dreamt he was waltzing, he kicked out his feet
And he kicked the bed-board from the bed.

One two three, balance like me…

Well after he practised a week or two
Sure he thought that he had it down fine
He went a lass and he asked her to waltz
He marched her straight out in the line,
He walked on her toes, he fractured her feet,
Sure he swore that her movements were false.
Poor girl she went round three weeks on a crutch
For teaching McFadden to waltz.

One two three, balance like me…

'Teaching McFadden to Waltz' has its origins in nineteenth century American vaudeville and music-hall entertainment. The original composition was 'Learning McFadden to Dance', by the New York songwriter M. F. Carey, who is better known for his song, 'You Can't Keep a Good Man Down'.[1] Carey was an arranger as well as lyricist and composer and his sheet music was distributed on both sides of the Atlantic thus spreading his popularity. When he composed this one in 1890 he dedicated it 'to the Gang', which might describe any cast for a music-hall show.[2] The key character in the Carey's song went by the name of Clarence McFadden, though once the song moved outside of the music-hall he turns up as Terence, and in Jerome's song his name is Charlie.

Apart from minor textual and melodic variations in Jerome's version, (not to mention the absence of piano accompaniment), the song still waltzes beautifully. It is understandable that Jerome would sing phrases that would feel more natural to him, such as 'bed-board' instead of 'dash-board' which he would reserve for cars. It is more curious that the version in Sean McMahon's *Irish-American Anthology* claims to be by 'Anon' yet is identical
to Carey's, word for word, though he used the title 'Teaching McFadden to Waltz'.[3]

Carey's original composition seems to have taken off in several directions, however, though not all of them could be attributed to the randomness of oral transmission. Some versions seem to have been skilfully re-crafted with the aim of cashing in on a good song.

Over several decades the song has been recreated for various forms of professional entertainment, particularly a silent move of the same title, released in New York in 1911. It starred two English-American actors, John Bunny (1863–1915), a larger than life character with very mobile facial expression, as McFadden, and Flora Finch (1867–1940) as his partner. Both excelled at boisterous comedy acting and, as Bunny weighed over 300 lbs and Finch was known as 'the skinny actress', the clumsy theme lent itself to their style.

In the 1930s it was recorded in London on a 78 rmp record, sung by Irish baritone, Sam Carson, to an orchestral accompaniment. According to Irish-American musician and writer Don Meade, "Sam Carson was the very Loyal Protestant alias of Samuel Greenfield, a doctor from Larne, County

---

[1] Listen on http://www.loc.gov/jukebox/recordings/detail/id/8638.

[2] Lester S. Levy Collection of Sheet Music, Department of Rare Books and Manuscripts, Sheridan Libraries, The Johns Hopkins University, http://levysheetmusic.mse.jhu.edu (Box 141, Item 169).

[3] McMahon introduces the song as "Late nineteenth-century proof of social climbing which was imported into Ireland and claimed as homegrown." See A *Little Bit of Heaven: An Irish-American Anthology,* pp. 82–83. Also, Roud 3707.

Antrim, who also recorded songs like 'McNamara's Band'... but altered the lyrics to remove some of the American flavor [sic]."[4] By most standards Carson has a good voice, but whatever the flavour, it does not mask the style of his singing, which (to my ear) is strident, overly staccato and, for this song, lacking in humour. Perhaps he is driven by the fast tempo set by orchestra, but it is doubtful that village hall dancers would get up for the waltz intended by the song.

There may have been no more curious re-creation of the song than 'One, Two, Three, I'll Teach You to Waltz', sung by Shirley Temple in the American film 'Susannah of the Mounties' (1939). Based on a Canadian novel of the same name, by Muriel Denison (1936),[5] in the American production the 'cutey-pie' star sings a reworked version of Carey's song as she waltzes. Despite close similarities in the lyrics, it has a new melody and is arguably a different song.[6]

A much more recent recording venture has well and truly claimed the song to be of Irish origin since the popular recoding duo 'Foster & Allen' have included it in a DVD entitled 'A Postcard from Ireland' (2006). Cashing in on the media that is particularly appealing to dollar tourists, the sales pitch can scarcely fail in terms of how people view themselves: "...amongst easy listening elite [the DVD] will allow the Irish community and loyal fans to enjoy the music and the countryside from Foster & Allen's homeland." For reasons better explained by the music business, the song now travels the world as 'Teaching McFadden to Dance' (though they actually *sing* 'waltz'). The song is virtually the same as Carson's version, though, sung to an accordion accompaniment, there is a warmer tone and suitable tempo for the waltz, which is performed (by actors) in a nostalgic Irish setting.

Jerome's version of the song is not the same as any of the commercial productions in either melody or lyrics. He sings, for example, 'you *aren't* quite a fairy', which makes more sense than 'you are quite a fairy', sung by the others, above-mentioned. His brother Joe recalls that Hughie O'Quinn used to sing it, and as they often got together, Jerome picked up the song from him. In view of the fact that Hughie, who was significantly older than Jerome, spent several years in Ireland, where he was in seminary training for the priesthood, the timing fits well with the release of Sam Carson's gramophone record. Hughie returned to the Valley with a broader education, which he put to excellent use, having decided that

---

[4] Though Meade was discussing one of Carson's other recordings, it also seems apt for 'Teaching McFadden to Waltz' as the 78 rmp recording affirms this suggestion – the song, as well as well as the voice, sounds 'straight from Ireland', as he intended. (http://www.youtube.com/watch?v=i08nrAX85-I) See, Don Meade's discussion in his paper, 'The Life and Times of "Muldoon, the Solid Man".

[5] The novel was set in Saskatchewan.

[6] The differences would comfortably avoid copyright issues with the Carey estate.

the priesthood was not his calling. Joe recalls that "Hughie had a hand in the song", and, this being so, the improvements to both words and tune serve it well. It also explains why 'Teaching McFadden to Waltz' does not appear to have been recorded elsewhere in Newfoundland, (even for the archives), as both singers were truly rooted in the Valley and neither sought fame or fortune through singing.

As Jerome was totally unconcerned by market issues or money-spinning potential, compared to those who have cashed in on such, his attitude as well as his singing is like a breath of fresh air. Accompanied by one foot, the song waltzes along in a steady tempo. It even has split-second pauses, which good dancers love, as they pause briefly on tiptoe before resuming their twirl around the floor. Every time Jerome sang it, like the skilled storyteller weighing each picture in words, he masterfully conveyed the comedy in his voice. As singers well know, they tread a very fine line between sounding as if they are about to laugh and actually laughing, which would not be desirable lest the song fall apart. Listeners to the CD will hear that Jerome succeeds, especially on the lazy, crazy line. And, as those who spent time in his company will testify, his eyes never failed to light up and shine with laughter every time he sang it.

Five Boss Highway[1]

Come all you boys from Codroy Valley who chance for to roam,
In search of employment go up on the road,
The Five Boss Highway, I'll give it full name,
I don't think I'm wrong, boys, for saying the same.

There's Mr Jim Tompkins, he's the head of the clan,
Right up to his shoulder is Sir Wallace Benn,
The other three bosses their names I'll reveal,
Mike Tompkins, Charlie Blanchard, and John M. MacNeill.

These men they are gentle in every way,
If the work it is hard, boys, these men you can't blame,
For there isn't one of those men will deny[2]
No man has the right for another to drive.

Oh that was the rule in the days of yore
Our great-grandfathers that are gone before
But it's not the custom to me or to you.
So we'll just drop the old rule and follow the new.

They started this contract one October day,
With axes and shovels they got on their way,
They'll hand them to you with their handles so fine
They'll make a man sweat, boys, or go down the line.

They're building this road about thirty feet wide,
They're putting a fine ditch up on each side
They built the camp buildings along by the road
And a big old cement can they're using for stove.

---

[1] Verses in italics are not on the CD as they are from the version sung by Martin Deveaux, also recorded in 1980, MUNFLA F3456/C4794. While the two sets of words are very similar, Martin sang two extra verses, (included here as 4 and 6) and he sang at a slightly brisker pace than Jerome.

[2] Martin Deveaux sang: 'But there is just one rule no man can deny'.

11. Five Boss Highway   95

When working on this road the accidents were few
And if you pay attention then I will tell you
There's no doctors, no nurses there, so assistance is slender
Con Benn cut his head and Jack Park cut his finger

While working on this job there was accidents too,
When Wally MacIsaac he went to the well
He fell in the bucket right up to his chin,
Put his elbow out of joint, 'twas a serious thing.

They all gathered round him and tied up his arm,
To Hughie MacIsaac they did give the alarm[3]
Put him in your dory this very day,
For MacKinnon's Shore you will steer your way.

Well the man on the survey I almost forgot
To tell you the truth he's the best of the lot
Only for his plans the roads would be spoiled,
He's a sport up Grand River, his name is Tom Doyle.

Oh they're giving this road up for winter days
You surely will smile if you went o'er that way.
For there were five bosses and only one man
And they had this poor fellow right down in the drain.

My song is now ended, I can't sing no more,
My tongue's getting tired, my throat's getting sore,
I hope you will take this all as a joke,
But it's no bloomin' wonder our government's broke.[4]

There may be no place on earth where road-making doesn't attract remarks, (usually wisecracks), or inspire songs, poems and tunes. Nevertheless, as early as 1834 the road-workers in Codroy Valley so impressed the government surveyor that they merited special mention in the House of Assembly in St. John's, where the Journal of April 19 records the report:

> We have marked instances of superiority of the road labour in that part of the country [Codroy Valley] as compared with other portions. I have no hesitation in saying that the superiority and

---

[3] Hughie MacIsaac was notified because he was Wally's father. Reflecting the Gaelic custom of using patronymics, Wally was known locally as 'Wally Hughie'.

[4] As was his style, Martin spoke the last line with considerable emphasis: 'But it's no goddam wonder our government's broke!

management is due entirely to the controlling genius of the one who has proved himself the guardian angel, as it were, of that part of the country since he has gone there. I refer to Monsignor [Thomas] Sears. So heartily are the people there alive to the development of their large agriculture resources that they have come forward manfully and subjected themselves to statute labour in order to open up new roads and keep the others in repair. This is a condition of affairs not realized in any other district of the Colony.[5]

Jerome's generation recall another very influential priest in the Valley, Monsignor Andrew Sears, a cousin of the first Monsignor Sears. Yet the memory of the earlier influence did not fade, as Jerome's brother Joe, a retired school-master, remarked that 'most of the early roadwork in the Valley was arranged by Monsignor *Thomas* Sears, parish priest from 1869–1885. I'm quite sure that the first land grants in the Valley came about as a result of his efforts.'[6]

By the late 1890s the railway from St. John's to Port aux Basques was complete, with stations at Doyles and St. Andrew's that could be accessed when necessary via unpaved roads and tracks that connected communities. As there was still a great need of a main road across Newfoundland, the Government implemented a scheme to improve communications. Once the survey was completed, the work was planned in sections, to be carried out over a number of years and supported by the Government's annual budget. This seasonal construction work became a source of income to fishermen, farmers and woodsmen whose picks and shovels built the highway over three generations. A huge undertaking by any standards, the main highway from St. John's to Port aux Basques was finally competed in 1966, by which time (27 years after Confederation) it had become part of the Trans-Canada Highway that stretched all the way to Vancouver.

As there are comparatively few communities situated right by the Highway, settlements in outlying areas were connected by a network of dirt roads, which, in the Codroy Valley, lasted until 1976, when the final stretch was paved. Aside from the minor annoyance of clouds of dust on dry summer days and the unexpected mud-slides of the spring thaw, these dirt roads were perfectly adequate and served communities well, particularly after the arrival of the motor-car.[7]

In July 1966, my first visit to Newfoundland taught me to appreciate these roads, as my father drove me from Gander airport to Marystown, on the southern tip of the Burin Peninsula. The journey began on the wide-

---

[5] *House of Assembly Journal*, April 19, 1834. See *The Last Stronghold*, p. 50. (My square brackets.)

[6] Joe Downey correspondence, March, 2012.

[7] The first car in the Valley was in 1921.

open Trans-Canada Highway, on which I felt a great sense of freedom as we breezed along miles of straight, smooth road, with ample room to pass. We stopped at a 'diner' to break the journey, and in some senses the 'news' that the next stretch of the journey would be a new experience – we were about to drive over a hundred miles of dirt road. I was soon to learn that this demanded an entirely different driving technique to the highway. Even although I grew up on an island with twisting single-track roads, with 'passing places' for on-coming cars, and the occasional mile of cart-track, this was no preparation for my first long journey on a dirt road.

Being a civil engineer (as well as a musician and yarn-spinner), my father regaled me with information the entire way, while I speedily wound up the window to keep out clouds of dust from on-coming cars. I would wind it down again for air after the dust had settled, as he'd begin another road-anecdote with, 'You have to understand,' followed by civil engineering information – the size of the 'bottoming' and where it had been quarried, the importance of the 'camber' to the driver, the co-efficient of expansion during freezing and thawing. I needed no more convincing: road-making is a big deal. So also is road-maintenance, and, having never seen a 'grader' until I went to Newfoundland, I was amazed at this formidable giant of a machine that slowly trundled along to remove ruts as well as the central ridge that accumulated from overuse – the young folk would say, "just don't get behind it" and old folk would reflect on how times had changed since their equipment consisted of a horse, cart and shovel.

The significance of such details to the song-maker or singer can only be appreciated in the context of the lives that were affected by the roads in question. The section of road that inspired Micky Jim to write 'The Five Boss Highway' is the stretch that is now regarded as the Exit to South Branch, about ten miles east of the main turn-off to the Codroy Valley.[8] Then, as now, construction workers were accommodated close to the site, as daily travel was impractical and, for some, impossible. The 'camp buildings along by the road' could be any construction site, even today, and the sort of ingenuity that turned a 'big old cement can' into a stove is still with us – keen campers pride themselves in being able to make a tin stove out of a bean-can.

As the road-making that occasioned Micky's song dates to the mid-1920s, when Jerome was only a small child, he had no personal experience of it, though he knew the men involved or their families. As Joe explained, the local gossip about some of the men is what lies behind Micky Jim's satire, so Jerome understood the irony in referring to Mr Tompkins as 'the head of the clan': "Maybe he didn't deserve it, but word had it he thought

---

[8] The location and its position in relation to the other communities can be seen on http://www.roadsidethoughts.com/nl/south-branch-map.htm. The stretch of highway under construction was 11 miles from Upper Ferry, where the song-maker Micky Jim MacNeil lived.

he was a cut above everyone else. And Wallace Benn gets called 'Sir' because he was like his henchman, his knight up to his shoulder!" Being a woodsman and hunter, Jerome knew of Tom Doyle, a well-liked man who had tourist camp on the Grand Codroy River. Such camps were, and are, highly rated and even the late King George was taken to one such camp for the salmon fishing.[9]

Jerome knew Micky Jim MacNeil quite well and enjoyed his company – "he lived over near Allan MacArthur." There were, however, a few of the older men in the Valley who could remember what the incident that sparked off the song, including Martin Deveaux,[10] who was in his late teens when construction began. Fifty years later he recalled what had taken place:

> That's when they cut the old highway, down near South Branch, at the Overfall … that was after the First World War, 1925 or 26. I learned the song from Mickey – he just lived next door to us. [He would have been around twenty-two at the time.][11]

Though neither Martin nor Jerome discussed the personalities involved, yet, the very mention of them evoked memories as well as general attitudes to life that still prevail. In a close-knit community such as this, it is important not to 'get above your station' or to display any hint of superiority, whether via personal wealth, ability or attitude. The first person mentioned in the song (Mr Jim Tompkins, the 'head of the clan') was, as it happens, the owner of one of the first cars in the Valley. That in itself would not cause resentment though undoubtedly all eyes would be on the owner as well as the new car. In today's terms, while it may be quite acceptable to own an impressive car, what is not acceptable is to try to impress others with it – the car can do that by itself, while the role of the owner is to 'make little of it' (or the money that bought it) and remain 'one of the boys (or girls)', unaffected by status or wealth. Meanwhile, it doesn't do be seen to keep in with folk who like to impress, as that was enough to earn Wallace Benn the satirical, if temporary, title of 'Sir'. As this is a fine line to tread, it is not surprising that not everyone succeeds.

While there is nothing explicit in the song to suggest whether Mr Tompkins was liked or disliked, Jerome's brother Joe recalled with some amusement that there seemed to be some tension between his grandfather and the man in question. Nevertheless, as has been proven time and time again, (particularly by couples who bicker or banter), some folk thrive on

---

[9] See, *The Last Stronghold*, pp. 28–29.

[10] The name now appears as Devoe, though the earlier Census Records all spell it *Deveaux*, the family being of French background. Martin was fluently bi-lingual and had several French songs in his repertoire.

[11] Recorded by K. Goldstein and M. Bennett, July 21, 1980.

such:

> Jim Tompkins and my grandfather, Tom Wall, seemed to always be at war with each other, or so the story goes. But when Jim Tompkins died in 1948, Tom Wall went to his wake and came out with tears in his eyes. Afterwards, a cousin of ours told me he was surprised at the sorrow on his grandfather's part. My response was, what would you expect when an Irish Warrior's last foe died? (Our grandfather, Tom, died in 1950.)

For decades after the Highway was complete the song still featured at house-parties and ceilidhs where it could spark off discussion or amusing anecdotes which, in turn, become part of the 'glue' that holds a community together. And Jerome, who kept the song alive, could still raise a smile, not only from men with experience of construction work but also from anyone who has ever seen a road-man lean on a shovel.

The Employment Song[1]

As I left home one morning employment for to find,
I thought I'd go and see the crowd upon the highway line,
Thinking I would be welcome as others of my kind
But when I heard them speaking I had to change my mind.

The only that I could hear as I went along
'Is that the young rascal composed the famous song?'
Then I went to the manager, these words to him did say:
'Shall I be numbered with the men that's hired here today?'

He pulled his shovel from the mud and stared at me in the face,
I didn't think a poet would work in such a dreadful place
Then after thinking between spells these words to me did say:
'Before I can hire you the timekeeper you must see.'

The timekeeper above the manager? I thought it very strange,
But like the English proverb says, 'Anything for a change.'
But he did not resemble one, by what I saw that day,
He used a pick instead of a pen, in the ditch he dug away.

He thought that I was sorry for making songs, I s'pose
But all the while my heart did smile, [as questions then arose]
Is it a disgrace for poets to work in place of misery
When managers and time-keepers are in up to the knees?

I do not want to criticise or otherwise abuse
But if a manager uses a pick-axe what should a labourer use?
I think I would be there yet, or p'haps until I die,
If I could not leave there without a definite reply.

The timekeeper he told me he knew what work was done
And to that information he'd go to no young one

---

[1] Verses in italics are form Martin Deveaux, MUNFLA

His memory must be bad, I think, if what I hear is right
For when you changed your course last fall we know of the result.

We have one consolation, the road you will not spoil
The superintendent overhauls the things that're not allowed
He visit here, when there is need, as an inspector would
But in the ditch up to his knees he's neither seen or heard.

I think that I have told you all that I heard and saw that day,
On my employment visit to the 'Five Boss Highway',
Is it a disgrace for poets to work in place of misery
When managers and timekeepers are in up to the knees?

I think that I have told you all that I heard and saw that day,
When on my employment visit to the 'Five Boss Highway',
'Twas the bosses in the ditches that really made me smile
All I can say, is <u>that I declare it really is a new style</u>![2]

For as long as Micky Jim MacNeil could remember, wordsmiths in the Valley had resorted to composing poems and songs of protest (Gaelic and English), as a way of drawing attention to social conditions and community concerns. Some were published in the weekly newspaper, *The Western Star*, such as scathing satire that appeared in 1904, after petitions for a telegraph office at Codroy had been ignored. It lashed out at the Premier of Newfoundland, Sir Robert Bond – addressing him as 'Mr' – to let him know he would lose their vote if he did not act on their behalf:

> We are twenty years behind the times
> And we know it to our cost;
> For the want of a telegraph office here
> Hundreds of dollars have been lost.
>
> Now Mr. Bond, of us you are fond
> Upon election day;
> We will, it's true, be fond of you
> If we get telegraphy.
>
> We now do stand each man to man
> With determination in view
> To gain some aid as to our needs
> Or vote no more for you![3]

---

[2] The underlined part of the line is spoken, rather than sung, by Martin Deveaux version. In his day, this was a common way of ending a song in the Valley as well as in other parts of Newfoundland.

[3] *The Western Star*, Aug. 31, 1904, verses 3, 4 and 7.

Though not all homes subscribed to a weekly paper, it was common to pass them on or to cut out 'clippings' to share at a ceilidh. It was all part of the way of life for Micky Jim who was in his early twenties when he composed the 'Five Boss Highway'. Given the fact that, in a community as close knit as the Valley all nine men named would soon have heard they had been mentioned, if not immortalised, in song, it might seem rash of him, even unwise, to have released the song in the first place. His next-door neighbour, Martin Deveaux, who learned the song as a teenager and continued to sing it for at least sixty years, explained how it came about: "After he made his first song, the men heard it, and they got sore. And then when Micky went out to look for a job, they wouldn't give him any! So he came home and he made another one!" Then, laughing, Martin took up the story in song: "As I left home one morning..."[4]

In the context of the community, the song documents an episode, which continues to be remembered as long as the song is sung. Among those who remember even one of the men named, or a relative, the song has the potential to spark off a discussion or initiate an amusing anecdote. Meanwhile, the song-maker is not by any means regarded as someone to be wary of, but continues to be recognized for his wit and humour as well as his ability as a song-maker.

---

[4] The core verses are almost identical to Jerome's; MUNFLA F3456/C4794

I Am a Roving Peddler

I am a roving peddler,
I've peddled in twin towns
Whenever I show a bag of spuds
I get my money down.

I've peddled down in Port aux Basques,
I've peddled in Grand Bay,
And I'd peddle o'er in Isle aux Mort,
If I only knew the way.

I've peddled in Mouse Island
Where the charming women dwell,[1]
Where they love the blue potato
And the cabbage just as well.

I see those ladies coming,
A-showing every curve,
And I'm so afraid they'll beat me down,
I almost lose my nerve.

My spuds they are two-seventy,
My turnip four a pound,
And my cabbage green as you've ever seen,
And I guarantee them sound.

Oh Johnny are they blue ones,
The ones so nice and dry?
The whites we get from the PEI[2]
Are watery like my eye.

I never had a failure,

---

[1] On another recording Jerome sang 'I've peddled in Mouse Island where the great big women dwell.'

[2] As Prince Edward Island prides itself as being Canada's 'spud island', Hughie may have been having a friendly dig at the neighbours across the Gulf.

I always sold my crop,
I peddle for my neighbour
And I peddle for the shop.

Now I've been promoted,
Oh, now I ride in style,
With the ex-chief in the driver's seat
The new chief buys the oil.

And now my song is ended,
I think I've done well,
Executives take me along
When they have anything to sell.

Before singing, Jerome introduced the song with: "It was composed by Hughie O' Quinn about 1960. It's not a very old song." The tune, however, is older and will be familiar to anyone who listened to popular music radio stations in the Fifties or Sixties – it brings to mind at least two 'hits', one by the Brothers Four and the other by Marty Robbins. As Hughie followed the tradition of choosing well known melodies that suited the sentiment of his compositions, this song fits the pattern so well that when (without explanation) I played the recording to the well-known American singer Skip Gorman, he sang along with Jerome for a verse and half before breaking into a surprised smile. The song in Skip's repertoire had a different context, but there were enough immediately recognisable elements that he was able to come straight in with his cowboy version, featuring the same tune and style:

> I am a roving gambler
> I've gambled all around,
> And wherever I see a deck of cards
> I lay my money down.[3]

On the surface, the composition is about a farmer from the Valley who loads his pick-up truck with locally grown vegetables, drives to communities a mere 25 miles away, and sells them round the houses and to grocery stores. (The 'twin towns' were two adjacent fishing ports, Channel and Port aux Basques, which were incorporated into the town of Channel-Port aux Basques in 1945. Since the 1970s the town has included the neighbouring settlements of Grand Bay East,

---

[3] Thanks to Skip Gorman for sharing the song as well as many more comparisons, such as 'I've gambled down in Washington, I've gambled up in Maine', etc. (In conversation, Perthshire, May 2012. Skip's style can be seen on www.skipgorman.com)

Grand Bay West and Mouse Island, which also features in the song.)

All seems to be going well until the farmer (Hughie himself) loses his driving licence and has to hire someone else to drive. When that happens, and he is relegated to the passenger seat, he makes light of the episode by referring to it as a promotion for the ex-chief. Or, as Jerome's brother Joe recalled, "Hughie got drunk ... it was round about the time he'd go selling vegetables down in Isle aux Mort and round the shore. And he lost his license..." There is warmth in Joe's voice and laughter in his eyes at the memories evoked by hearing the song – a story comes to mind, and though it is a variant of the anecdote Dan MacArthur told [p. 59], it bears re-telling as such stories reflect the wit of the tellers as well as their subject:

> I'm not sure Hughie was on a selling mission that time he was stopped – he was in Corner Brook, going the wrong way a one way street. There was a little matter of too much refreshment and the policeman who stopped him said, "Sir, this is a one way street."
> And Hughie answered, "I'm only going one way!"
> And he lost his license, so he kind of handed the business over to his pal. He still of course dictated the terms![4]

Forty years after Hughie composed it, the song is still a lively talking point in the Valley, with reminiscences that usually began, "I remember one time," or "only last year..." Stories seem to sprout out of Hughie's song, each with its own take on the subject, with least attention allocated to the driving offence, which is frequently ignored or dismissed with: "that could happen to anyone." More important for the story are economic considerations for the farmers, such as Jerome's contemporary, Leo Cormier, who could appreciate the hard work that goes into growing, thinning and harvesting, as well as in marketing farm produce. Long after he had retired, one of Leo's kitchen yarns (told between songs) involved one of trying to sell turnips in Port aux Basques in the 1970s. By that time 'chain' supermarkets had been set up and, as they imported produce from across the Gulf, Leo reached a gloomy conclusion for local growers: "Pretty near had to give 'em away for all you'd get for them, and by the time I was through I hardly made enough money to cover the gas..."

While the 'Roving Peddler' begins in the Valley, the song takes in communities lying on the south-west coast of Newfoundland. A glance at the map shows that Channel-Port aux Basques is only 25 miles away from where Hughie lived, in today's terms, a short drive. From there, Isle aux Morts is about 30 miles along the coast. Yet the song cannot be understood by looking at the road map as it gives no context whatsoever for the experience of the 'peddler' or of the folk who bought his produce.

---

[4] DVD 2007.

There can be few neighbouring landscapes more contrasting than the Codroy Valley, the 'Garden of Newfoundland', and the windswept, rocky settlements along the south-west coast. One area supports farmers, the other fishermen, and between them is the windiest stretch of road imaginable, which closes when gales up to Force 10 blow cars and trucks off the road and trains off the track.[5] Since anyone can remember, only one house has stood there, the one-story 'Wreck House', home of Mr & Mrs Lauchie MacDougall, who relied on a crank telephone to send out warnings.[6] But even in the most clement weather, nothing can be taken for granted, in terms of how people survived, far less made a living.

The fertile alluvial plane stretching the length of the Valley can produce an abundance of fresh vegetables and soft fruits, as well as grain and hay to support the biggest herd of dairy cows in Eastern Canada. The south-west coast is another matter, for, picturesque as it is, it has taken years to carve out the modern town settlement that tourists see today.

In February 1949, a month before Newfoundland became Canada's tenth province, the area was featured in a magazine article entitled, 'ATLANTIC GUARDIAN visits the twin towns of Channel and Port aux Basques'. The tone is lively and positive as the reporter describes the progress that has taken place in the town:

> ... the existence of the town of Channel is a tribute to the courage and hardihood of its inhabitants for the little soil left there after the glacial period has long since been eroded... its raison d'être was codfish... Since their incorporation in 1945, the towns have made giant strides in civic improvement. The terrain is most difficult for road-making yet already one mile of modern road has been built with their own machinery ... [The report goes on to say that] some of the residents were beginning to plant gardens... and some have brought soil from twenty miles for this purpose...[7]

One mile of modern road! This is the port where today's tourists arrive from mainland Canada or the States, ready to experience Newfoundland. They will not be disappointed if they have come for the scenery, hunting, fishing or unmatched hospitality; but, as they drive off the ferry in giant motor homes, cars or pick-trucks, few might have any idea of the road that would have welcomed them sixty years ago.

---

[5] For a recent example, see the news report: www.cbc.ca/news/canada/newfoundland-labrador/story/2008/05/22/wreckhouse-trucks.html.

[6] An automated station now issues weather warnings at Wreckhouse, which is one of Canada's official weather stations.

[7] *ATLANTIC GUARDIAN*, Vol. VI, No. 2, Feb. 1949, St. John's, Newfoundland, p. 39–40.

This was the Newfoundland that Hughie and his generation, as well as Jerome's, knew and cared about.[8] Even with the progress that had been attained by 1960, travel between settlements was far from easy, particularly to outports such as Isle aux Morts. There can be no doubt that the roving peddler was a welcome figure when he arrived, bringing with him vegetables that were impossible to grow locally. And, as was the custom among rural folk, hospitality went without saying – a cup of tea, a glass of home-brew, or just one for the road.[9]

From the point of view of those who lived along that coast, contact with the outside world was often difficult; but it was crucial to their survival. Few, if any, made a point of recording details of their day-to-day life, yet their memories live on, re-told by those who value them.[10] In this context, Hughie O'Quinn's song becomes a remarkably evocative document of social history: remembering communities which, even today, are considered off the beaten track. As folklorist Alan Dundes noted, "Folklore, [which includes songs], as a mirror of culture, provides unique raw material for those eager to better understand themselves and others."[11] And the many fireside discussions in the community that have been sparked off by this song play an important role in furthering that understanding.

---

[8] Hughie was in his mid-forties and Jerome was twenty-five when Newfoundland joined confederation.

[9] The pattern is familiar to anyone who remembers travelling salesmen in rural Scotland or Ireland. (My grandmother even made tea for the 'tea man' who travelled the Highlands of Scotland.) It also continues in my generation with the custom of making tea for workmen hired for domestic or garden work.

[10] In 1970 I recorded the former district nurse stationed east of Isle aux Morts at Grand Bruit. (MUNFLA C869/71-48.) Though the journey from St. John's took a week by boat (the only route), it was, nevertheless, easier than it is now as there is no longer any public transport to Grand Bruit since it was resettled in 2010. Evelyn said she went ashore to a place that seemed to cling to the cliffs. With scarcely any land to cultivate, vegetables were very scarce, in some places non-existent, which took a toll on general health. See, M. Bennett, 'So Many Steamers Ago: Memories of an English Nurse in Newfoundland in the 1930s' in *Essays in Lore and Language: A Festschrift for John Widdowson*, pp 22–42.

[11] Alan Dundes, *Interpreting Folklore*, p. viii.

The Galway Shawl

At Erinmore in the County Galway,
One pleasant evening in the month of May,
I spied a damsel, she was fair and handsome,
Her beauty fairly took my breath away.

Chorus:
She wore no jewels, no costly diamonds,
No paint nor powder, no, none at all.
She wore a bonnet with a ribbon on it
And around her shoulder was the Galway Shawl.

As we kept on walking, sure she kept on talking,
Till her father's cottage came into view.
She said, "Come in, sir, and meet me father,
And play to please him 'The Foggy Dew'."

Well I played 'The Blackbird'
and 'The Stack of Barley',
'Old Rodney's Glory' and 'The Foggy Dew';
She sang each note like an Irish linnet.
And the tears stood in her eyes of blue.

'Twas early, early, all in the morning,
I started out for old Donegal.
She said 'Goodbye,' as she cried and kissed me,
But my heart remained with her Galway shawl.

Jerome became well known in the Valley for his wide repertoire of Irish songs, including this one, which had been a life-long favourite as he learned it from his father. In 2007, however, when I visited him after many years, the song took on an important significance: I had not been to Jerome and Rosie's since the 1990s, but when I eventually managed to get there (on a visit from my home in Scotland), Jerome had been diagnosed with Alzheimer's disease. "He won't know you," I was told, "he hasn't sung for a long time... it's doubtful if he could remember a song now." Somehow, it seemed all the more important to visit, if only to smile, touch his hand, kiss his cheek, offer a silent expression of gratitude to one who had given so much through his songs. Furthermore, a visit with Rosie was equally important, for she had always been by his side, his daily companion sharing his life of songs.

The welcome was as warm as ever, as Rosie quietly led us though the kitchen to where Jerome was seated, silently looking out of the window. But within minutes of hearing our conversation, he looked directly at me and said, "I know you, we used to sing!"

"We certainly did," was my response, pulling my chair closer (while locating my mini-disc and microphone). "All those favourites ... 'The Star of Logy Bay' and 'The Black Velvet Band'... 'Two Little Girls in Blue'... Lots of songs, Jerome... how about singing 'The Galway Shawl'?" And with a smile, he began, melodious and expressive as ever, the entire song without any hesitation. In his singing of this and other songs, Jerome revealed far more than mere information about where a song originates – does that really matter? Much more significant was his demonstration of how little we know about the human mind, the role of memory and the place of song in retaining it. And what of instrumental music?

"Jerome, how about a tune? You used to play the fiddle and the accordion!"

"Oh, I believe I did! But it's been a long time...."

The fiddle was taken down from the hook on the wall, the accordion located and laid beside him. Then, perched on the edge of his chair with the fiddle across his arm, he played. Then, picking up the button-melodeon, Jerome not only retained the tunes accurately, but, in playing 'Scotland the Brave' for his Scottish visitor, he still demonstrated a strong perceptive awareness of his audience. While instrumental musicians sometimes speak of 'muscle memory' the term tends to belong to the domain of neurobiologists. Of that science I know nothing, save what Jerome taught me: music and song have a profound role to play in the study of the human mind.

Meanwhile, there is no definitive information about the origin of 'The Galway Shawl', which turns up the world over and in many variants. Probably the earliest 'collected' version was from Bridget Kealey, Dungiven, County Derry who sang it in 1936 for Sam Henry's newspaper column, 'Songs of the People' in the *Northern Constitution*.[1] The song also caught

---

[1] The newspaper was published in Coleraine and the column, which began in 1923, was so popular that it ran until 1939. See, *Sam Henry's Songs of the People*, p. 269. Roud 2737.

on in England and Scotland, not only among Irish immigrants but also among the travelling people who spent seasons in Ireland.[2]

As new anthologies of songs appear, as well as digital collections, there may be few songs more discussed than 'The Galway Shawl'. Some singers (or are they listeners?) find it too sentimental, while others persist in their quest for an 'original' model. Granted, the text seems to have the ring of a broadside ballad, yet there seems to be no song listed in the many archive holdings. Nevertheless, certain enthusiastic (but anonymous) song detectives have tracked it down and agree that it is based on an older Broadside Ballad, 'The Red Plaid Shawl' by an unknown composer. Copies of this broadside turn up on both sides of the Atlantic, but, as all are undated, with no indication of place of origin, there is little left to say – except perhaps that, if texts are anything to go by, I'd sooner have the Galway Shawl any day than the Red Plaid. Shawls, like songs, are simply a matter of taste.

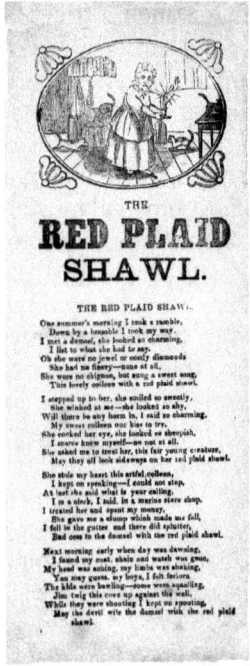

Courtesy of Lester S. Levy Collection of Sheet Music, Department of Rare Books and Manuscripts, Sheridan Libraries, The Johns Hopkins University, http://levysheetmusic.mse.jhu.edu.

---

[2] See, for example, the version from the Stewarts of Blairgowrie recorded by Ewan MacColl and Peggy Seeger, *Till Doomsday in the Afternoon*, pp. 218–220.

Mary Kate White

Gussie Gale from Millville is one of the boys
Sure he's out in the Backlands engaged, cutting ties;
You can hear his axe ringing from morning till night;
And then he goes courting young Mary Kate White.

Oh Phil was her father with knitting to do,
So he says then unto Gussie, 'I'll give it to you,
You can take it to Paul Joseph's and get it done up,
    why it won't take him long,
And on your return you can bring it along.[1]

Neddy was her sweetheart, he had his foot cut,
And now says young Gussie 'I will do my stuff,'
He took her to Millville down to a card game,
But little he thought it was labour in vain.

It was on a Thursday evening, Fanny said to Phil,
"We have a bag of wool down at the mill".
So up spake Phil, and he makes Katie blush,
Why he said, "'Tis your own fault,
    you should have told Gus."

It was on a Sunday evening he shouldered the bag
From Millville to the Backlands it is quite a drag.
From shoulder to shoulder, from left to the right
Why he didn't let up till he reached Placide White's.

He looked at the clock, sure the hour being late,
It was far too late for to see handsome Kate.
So he picked up the bag and he hugged it goodnight,
Saying, "If it were Katie my heart would be light."

Oh, then early next morning he first ate his fill,
Then he picks up the bag and he beat it for Phil's.

---

[1] Though this is the only verse of the song with an extra phrase in the second line, Jerome sings it with agility and revels in the element of surprise it adds to the song.

If you had been there, you would laugh your skin full,
To see him 'fore daylight going off with his wool.

Now Neddy's foot is better, he is doing the rush.
So now he and Katie they play cards for Gus.
At five cents a corner the price it is small,
Whoever gets Gussie will have a nice doll.

Now Neddy's foot is better, 'Your good times are gone,
So tend to your tie-cutting up at Goose Pond.
Although you're so long, sure so broad and so stout,
Sure, 'tis not in your britches to cut Neddy out![2]

Jerome learnt this song from Paul Hall, who composed it about 1935 when Mary Kate White would have been seventeen, Jerome twelve and Paul himself thirty-seven. Combining two universal themes of 'all's fair in love and war,' and 'you can't blame a fellow for trying', the song is so local and of its time that perhaps it might not have been expected to outlive the key characters.

It may seem surprising, then, that more seventy years on, Jerome not only sang it, but, on occasions, would also be requested to sing it. As he never lost the freshness of each performance, his engagement with both song and audience had potential to open up discussion, particularly among those too young to have known that generation. And, as everyone loves romance (if not gossip), some would be curious as to which particular family all the participants came from – especially since, when Paulie composed the song in 1935, on the stretch of road where he lived, six out of ten houses belonged to a family of Gales.[3] Following the advent of on-line censuses, there has been an upsurge of interest in genealogy and family history; so now, for the real enthusiasts zealously looking for the next clue to fill in a blank, there is an opportunity to join the discussion.

On the surface, the song may have a fairly thin plot, although to imagine what Gussie was doing the uninitiated may need to know that 'ties' are nothing to do with smart clothing: After the trees were felled and sawn into length, the skilled woodsmen used a broad-axe to square the logs into beams, or 'ties', such as railroad ties. At a deeper level, however, it contributes to the social history of the Valley. While nobody (except perhaps the priest) spoke publicly about the boundaries of courtship, it was widely accepted that there were certain social and moral expectations, which were generally followed. Asking a girl to go out on a date usually took the form of inviting her to a socially visible event such as a card game, where, in the company of other people, they could be near one

---

[2] Leonard's version (2012) as 'It's not in your power to cut Neddy out.'

[3] They are all listed in the 1935 Newfoundland Census, St. George's District.

another. Card games and cribbage are still a common feature of the social life of the Valley, and, as often as not couples are invited for an evening, sometimes on a 'turn about' basis. Getting together for a light-hearted game (sometimes played with small coins or even match sticks as the stake) gives folk a chance to catch up on local news, fill a glass or two and forget about the day's drudgery. Around the kitchen table, which will later be cleared for tea and a 'lunch', there is always banter and humour, teasing and laughter, jokes and wisecracks and occasional flirting; all enjoyed as 'good clean fun'.

Moral expectations are discussed in terms of anecdotes (told as true, sometimes naming someone in the company), such as this one:

> Anyway, this fellow, he says, "Now we've been out together a few times and it's been pretty good, eh? So, do you think we should get married or what?"
> And she says to him, "There'll be no 'or what' *unless* we're married!"

The ensuing laughter is the cue for one of the older generation to tell the young: "That was how it was in our day, that's for sure. And we walked everywhere…" From that point, were I to re-write the script it could be based on facts drawn from the song and numerous conversations, corroborated with precise evidence of a local map and the Newfoundland Census of 1935.

To set us straight, Kenny Goldstein asked Jerome where Paul Hall lived, and, as we were in Jerome and Rosie's home at the time, he replied: "Well, he lived in Millville, down the road from here [Great Codroy], about three and a half, four miles," [west, see map]. When Paul was young, O'Regans used to be known as the 'Backlands'[4] and that's where Gussy [Augustus] Gale was cutting ties. The first house at the end of the road belonged to a family of Ryans, then there was another family of Ryans, and next door were the Farrells, then another house and the next again was where Mary Kate White lived. Her father was Phil (he's in the song) and her mother was Frances (Fanny, they called her), then next-door but one was Neddy, Edward or Ned Ryan – he lived with his aunt and uncle who were up in years.

Now, Gussy Gale, he's Isidore Gale's son, and that family lived about a mile past Paulie Hall's place. But before you get there, just the next house to Paulie Hall was Paul Joseph O'Quinn – he had a knitting machine, "he would use it on the kitchen table, the kind that would go back and forth, by hand, because there was a lot of knitting to be done in those days."[5] And

---

[4] See, 'Place Name Changes for St. George's District' (http://ngb.chebucto.org/Name-Changes/stg-nc.shtml).

[5] MUNFLA 88-226. During fieldwork in 1969, Mrs Allan (Mary) MacArthur demonstrated a mechanical knitting machine that she bought via a mail-order

he also used to be good at mending things. So Gussy would stop at Paul Joseph's on the way to see his own family. And once he got there, the very next house was the Gales who owned the mill – one of the sons took over from his father and he ran it till it closed down. So it must be a good eight miles from Mary Kate White's to the mill – that's a long way to ask anyone to carry a bag of wool! It could be pretty heavy because one fleece weighs between 5 and 10 pounds and Phil had quite a few sheep. Now, who would have thought some fellow would walk eight miles carrying a big bag of wool because he fancied your grandmother? And he had to go twice!

Such is the gist, and though listeners in the Valley – even those from the other side of the river – would not be expected to know every family, they are not excluded from the conversation. Memories are evoked, anecdotes are told, and further discussion may arise. For some of the participants it is like piecing together a jig-saw, and if the evening ends with patches of landscape unfinished the puzzle may be picked up later. It is not unusual for follow-up phone calls with fresh clues ("I was just talking to Mom about...") or even an email such as this one from Joe:

> Up to the time of Confederation, the carding mill was important in the valley. The chief source of power for the mill was a water wheel in Grand Daddy's Brook. When I was in the mill twice around 1945–47, there was also a gasoline engine, which ran some of the equipment. There was also another carding mill operated by David Lomond (yes, the same man who became game warden in 'Come All Ye Jolly Hunters'). This mill did not have the success that the Gale mill had. At the Gale mill the product was 'rolls' used to spin yarn.[6] They would buy your wool or card it and take enough to pay for the carding.
>
> In my memory, Edward Gale, Afra's brother, ran the carding mill. After confederation the mill did not provide him with a living, and he went into other things. (In the mid fifties, highway construction jobs were plentiful and "Ned" worked as a flagman.) There was a big change when we entered confederation. I can list three reasons for the changes.
>
> 1) With confederation came family allowance, which put money in the pockets of the really poor people; and then in 1952 everyone who had attained the age of seventy received the old age pension. I think it was forty dollars a month at first.
>
> 2) The value of wool decreased, probably because more synthetic materials were used.

---

catalogue from the States. It was a small circular device with needles and hooks, on which she made socks, sleeves for sweaters, and legs for long-johns. (Fieldwork notebook, 1969). See also M. Bennett, *Oatmeal and the Catechism*, pp. 201–211.

[6] Mary MacArthur described spinning the 'rollags/ at spinning bees, which were once common all over The Valley. see, The Last Stronghold, pp.148-52.

3) Many people sent their wool to Charlottetown, PEI to be carded. They made the wool into yarn and also products such as blankets and socks. They would also buy the wool and/or buy enough to pay for the services rendered.

Afra and his wife[7] ran the post office. He was also a tin smith and operated a saw mill. In its early days the saw mill was also powered by a water wheel on Granddaddy's Brook. The carding mill that David Lomond had was at least partially powered by a water wheel. [8]

Such are Joe's bright memories, that flood back with the song sung by his brother. As I listen again to 'Mary Kate White', I begin to recall an old house I once rented for fieldwork nearly forty years ago – it was one of O'Quinns in Millville, an elderly man, Paul Jospeph, who had moved to be with family. Jerome and Joe would have known him. And sure enough, though Joe's confirmation was not quite the 'yes' or 'no' I had anticipated, I soon learned:

Paul Joseph O'Quinn was one of the bootleggers referred to in Paul Hall's song:
The names of those bootleggers I'll tell you them all.
Paul William, Paul Joseph and young Paulie Hall.[9]
The fines those gentlemen had to pay were not large; but Paul Joseph decided it was too much to pay, so he would serve the gaol time. He found the time too tough, so he asked to have the fine paid. His mother arranged to pay the fine in pennies.[10]

Bootleggers? Now there's a story! I wonder if anyone knows the song? Meanwhile, just for the records, on July 18, 1938, Edward James Ryan (31) married Mary C. White (20) of O'Regans at St. Ann's Catholic Church.[11] I wonder, though, who got the 'nice doll'?

---

[7] In 1970 Afra Gale showed me the carding mill and demostrated how the machines operated, MUNFLA C870/71-48. See. *The Last Stronghold*, p. 148.

[8] To make sure the transcribed text was accurate, I sent it to Joe ((May 13, 2012). When he emailed his response it was evident that even reading the text of a song was enough to stir the memory; so, for this reason, with his permission, I include it verbatim.

[9] Joe refers to another song here.

[10] Correspondence with Joe Downey, May 2012.

[11] St. Ann's RC Parish Marriage Records (http://nl.canadagenweb.org/wcod_marr_stannes1.htm) Not all the records remain, as there was a serious fire which destroyed many of them. See, *The Last Stronghold*, p. 196, endnote 12.

Paddy Hagerty's Old Leather Britches

At the sign of a bell on the road to Clonmel
Paddy Hagerty kept a neat shebeen;
He sold pig's feet and bread, kept a neat lodging bed
Round the county well known, sure he had been.
There Pat and his wife they struggled through life
On the weekdays they mended the ditches,
On Sunday he dressed in a coat of the best
But his pride was his old leather britches.

For twenty-one years, or so it appears,
Pat's father did britches hand-running;
When he was dying and on his bed lying
Called Paddy his dutiful son in.
Advice that he gave as he went to his grave,
"I'll have you take care of me riches –
I'm weary to choose you step into me shoes
But I'll have you step into my britches."

With last winter's snow provisions got low
And Paddy got ate out completely;
With the snow coming down Pat could not get to town
Thoughts of hunger soon bothered him greatly.
One night as he lay a-dreaming away
Of fairies and cross dogs and witches
He heard an uproar outside of the door
He jumped up and hauled on his britches.

Sure then in great haste to the doorway he made
Still dreaming of cross dogs and witches
Said big Andy Moore, "Break open the door
For this is no night to be waiting!"
The word was scarce spoke when the door it was broke
And they all flocked round Paddy like leeches,
Saying "You great mortal hog, if you don't give us prog
We'll eat you right out of your britches!"

Then Paddy in fear to his bedroom repaired
Called Judy his own darling wife in,
'Twas there they agreed they would have a feed
So he went out and brought the long knife in.
He caught hold of the base of the britches, in haste,
Sure he cut off the buttons and stitches,
He cut them in strips and he swore it was tripe,
And he boiled them his old leather britches.

And when it was stewed, around it they stood
Then the boys all they cried, "Lord, we thank ye."
Then Hagerty's wife, for fear of her life,
She thought it high time for to shank it.
As they messed on the stuff, says Andy "Tis tough",
Says Darby, "You're no judge of mutton";
When Brian MacGurk on the point of his fork
Held up a large ivory button.

"Oh what is that, Pat?" "Oh I thought it was fat!"
He jumped on his legs and he screeches,
"By the powers above I was trying to shove
Me teeth through the flap of his britches."
Oh, for vengeance they took all his platters they broke,
They broke all his pots, pans and dishes,
And from that very night they'd break out your daylight
If they caught you wearin' old leather britches!

Jerome learned this song from his grandfather, Michael Downey, who was born in 1861 and known locally as 'Long Mike'. The fact that he died in 1935, when Jerome was only twelve, is evidence of how young Jerome was when he learned 'Grandfather's song', as he called it. No matter how often he sang it, however, the story seemed to unfold anew, and, with remarkable freshness, Jerome's sense of humour would shine at each singing. His timing impeccable, he would weigh anew moments of suspense to fit the details of the 'plot', and, with eyes twinkling, he would convey laughter in his tone of voice. This was also one of several songs that reflected Jerome's sense of pride in his family roots, for only the Irish, or the Irish-Newfoundlander, could do justice to a song such as this. This was, and is, well recognised the Valley, where younger generations of singers still reflect their family backgrounds in their choice of songs, retaining the rich variety that has always been enjoyed at sing-arounds and get-togethers.

Comic songs that delight in indulging a sheer sense of the ridiculous have long been championed by the Irish. Many, such as this one, date to the nineteenth century, the hey-day of music-hall as well as street singers and broadside ballad sellers who frequented markets and fairs all over Ireland. Jerome's song is a variant of 'Paddy Hagerty's Leather Breeches', published in London by W.S. Fortey, 'sometime between 1858 and 1885'.[1] As is usually the case with these penny broadsheets, there is no record of the composer's name and no music, though some are 'to the tune of...'

To the Gaelic ear, however – Irish or Scottish – the style is instantly identifiable by the *internal* rhymes and assonance throughout. In the first line we hear 'bell' rhyming with 'Clonmel', rapidly followed by the phrases 'pig's feet and bread' and 'neat lodging bed' (with the same number of syllables in each). English language poets seek rhyming words to end their lines, but not so with the Gaelic bards, who, from the ancient past to more modern times honed their skill in internal rhyme, which characterizes the poetry and song of the true Gael. Irish writer and broadcaster Seán O Boyle, commissioned by the BBC to make field recordings of Ulster folk music for a radio series 'As I Roved Out' (1952 to 1954), discussed the phenomenon in his book, *The Irish Song Tradition*. Songs of this kind were 'written in English, but following closely the metrical laws of Irish, imitating as closely as the English Language allowed...'

> [Such] songs based on the Irish metres became favourites with itinerant ballad singers who, by the end of the nineteenth century, had replaced the wandering harper' as the source of entertainment and of new songs... Many of these the ballad singer hawked through the fair, market, football matches, race meetings and political gatherings, songs on every theme of love, courtship, emigration [and so on].[2]

In both Ireland and Scotland there are numerous examples of modern bards whose compositions seem to reverse the process as far traditionalists are concerned – they make Gaelic poems and songs that seem inert rhythmically, and furthest removed from what are recognised as 'traditional meters'. As Gaelic scholar Dr John MacInnes remarked, when he first heard an example of this kind of Gaelic poetry (which seemed quite unsingable), one of the older bards said [in Gaelic], "That's only English poetry written in Gaelic!"[3] While this style may be viewed as accelerating a decline in Gaelic tradition, the nineteenth century English songs that 'played' with Gaelic meter are much more entertaining.

---

[1] National Library of Scotland digital archives: http://digital.nls.uk/english-ballads/pageturner cfm?id=74891644. See also, The Bodleian Library of Broadside Ballads, Oxford University, shelfmark: Harding B 11(2915). Roud 923.

[3] *The Irish Song Tradition* (Dublin, 1976), pp. 14–15.

[3] Dr John MacInnes, in conversation, used with permission, 2012.

The opening line of 'Paddy Hagerty's Old Leather Britches' establishes the pattern, then the song takes off, retaining the style throughout, apart from one minor exception, verse 5 line 7, when Jerome sings 'He cut them in *strips* and he swore it was tripe' – that makes sense, where no combination of strips, stripes, trips or tripes would work, or make sense, which was always important to Jerome. The hack writer of the original who got paid so much a song by the printer, however, could get away with an odd line such as 'He cut them in stripes and he swore it was tripes', disregarding the sense for the sake of the internal rhyme and general amusement. In Ireland, as in Scotland, there was also a certain mileage to be gained in making fun of Gaelic speakers with an incomplete command of English.[4]

Irish piper, printer and song collector Colm Ó Lochlainn, who included a version entitled 'The Old Leather Breeches' in his anthology *Irish Street Ballads*, describes songs in this style as belonging to 'the half-way house between Irish culture and the new English way.'[5] Given the centuries-long connection between Newfoundland and Ireland, it is not surprising that so many of them have become part of the Newfoundland-Irish repertoire. Though this one also turns up in Kenneth Peacock's *Songs of the Newfoundland Outports*, (recorded in St. John's in 1952)[6], Jerome's version is actually much closer to that collected in Ireland by Ó Lochlainn. As he sings it with a masterful sense of timing, the story develops with all its hilarity while Jerome shares his glowing sense of enjoyment.

---

[4] This is very common among Scottish Gaels, who use elements of literal translation for amusement, e.g. 'He tore his new trouser' would raise a laugh, as the word for this item of clothing is singular in Gaelic, whereas in English the 's' renders it plural. The listener may decide which is the more logical word for a single item of clothing.

[5] *Irish Street Ballads*, Introduction, p. xi. The song appears as Number 67A in the Appendix, pp. 214–5. The famous Behan family also sang a version, 'The Oul Leather Britches', song 66 in Dominic Behan's book, *Ireland Sings*.

[6] Entitled 'Leather Britches', it was sung by from Gordon Willis (1911-001) and appears in Volume 1, pp. 71–2. It was also recorded in Nova Scotia by Helen Creighton as 'Paddy Hagerty's Breeches' sung by Fred Redden of Middle Musquodoboit; the tape is archived in the Nova Scotia Archives, (Rec no. 2962, Loc. no. AR 5779, AC 2204, MF no. 289.631).

Come All Ye Jolly Hunters

Come all ye jolly hunters who
are gathered here today.
Come all ye jolly hunters
and listen to me, pray.
I'll sing for you a little song;
in fact, I will relate
It happened in the later part
of nineteen fifty-eight.

There is a man in our town,
Leonard Hynes it is his name;
To shoot a bird upon the wing,
he's noted for his fame.
We have another man, you know,
Walter Gale we'll call him here,
A stout young man of noble heart,
he shows so little fear.

Dave Lomond is our river guard,
and boys, you'd best watch out,
For it's a mighty crime, you know,
to shoot a harmless goose.
But word got out that evening
that Dave was heading east,
So those two lads they started out
to get themselves some geese.

They got a boat and started out
on a cold December day
To get themselves some fresh meat
to serve on Christmas Day.
They travel o'er the water where
the long-necked chickens roam,
But on that very evening,
why, Dave did come home.
Oh Rachael was the first one

to meet him at the door,
Saying, "Dave, oh my darling,
there's someone on the shore!"
Said Dave to his loving wife,
"Oh Rachael, may I ask,
If it's someone from St Andrews
or are they from Port aux Basques?"

Oh, Dave he got ready then
to travel through the snow
To go to St Andrews
and let the Mounties know.
He dressed himself and started out
in the bitter wind and cold,
And when he reached the officers
the story to them told.

The Mounties came all on the run,
old Rankin arrived on time,
To prosecute the murder
of such a drastic crime.
Pete Moriarty was the second,
as you've already heard,
To prosecute the murderer
of such a precious bird.

They travelled down to our town
on a cold December day,
With Dave in the front seat
to guide them on their way.
They travelled to the crossroads,
as you already know,
Where they picked up the tyre tracks
in the newly-fallen snow.

Oh, they arrived at Leonard's gate
a quarter after three,
Where those two lads had stopped to have
themselves a cup of tea.
But Rankin did not falter,
he rapped upon the door,
Where Mrs Hynes was serving tea –
it made her rather sore.

Now this is the end of my story, boys,
I hope it's not a crime,
I hope I have offended none
or wasted your precious time.
But here's to all you hunters,
oh, come you one and all,
And I hope that you have better luck
in the coming fall!

Although the Festive Season has always been special, going to Port aux Basques to buy a big turkey is relatively recent, compared to the days when a wild goose or duck from the Valley was a more common Christmas dinner. Hunting was a way of life for Jerome, who learned the song in 1958: "I just heard somebody singing it and I picked it up. I knew the people that were involved, so I just heard it and sang it."

As far as he knew, it was composed by a group of local lads, none of whom wished to claim authorship any more than they wished to get on the wrong side of the game warden. He was a perfectly nice fellow, but he was still the game warden. The tune, being a variant of the Irish rebel song 'Johnson's Motor Car', suggests that 'the boys' enjoyed being party to the illegal escapade that occasioned their song.

Hunting and fishing are serious business in the Valley, as wild meats have always been part of the diet, once out of necessity and now out of choice. The earliest tour-guide books for Newfoundland single out the Codroy Valley as being a sportsman's paradise – even the late King George was taken there on a salmon fishing expedition. Game hunting and salmon fishing are not (as in Scotland) mainly for landlords and wealthy visitors but, as any Newfoundlander will testify, when the hunting season approaches, hardly a day goes by without someone asking if you got your licence.

Besides the big game (moose, caribou and black bear) there are a number of smaller animals and wild birds, including migratory geese, which may be hunted or trapped by holders of the appropriate licence. The rules are widely known but, as frequently happens elsewhere too, some are 'made to be broken' by otherwise law-abiding citizens. My grandfather once explained to me (in response to a question about a salmon) that, "The good Lord put the salmon in the river before these fools made the rules."

As it is never a good idea to get on the wrong side of the game warden, there is usually a protective silence when it comes to giving information about poachers. And in this song, the silence extends to the song-makers themselves, who would rather not be named. You never know, after all, when someone might make a song about you.

The Cameron Men

There's many a man in the Cameron Clan
That has followed his Chief to the field;
He has sworn to support him or die by his side,
For a Cameron never can yield.

Chorus:
I hear the pibroch sounding, sounding,
Deep o'er the mountain and glen,
While light-springing footsteps are trampling the heath,
'Tis the march of the Cameron men.
'Tis the march, 'tis the march,
'Tis the march of the Cameron men.

The moon has arisen, it shines on the path
Now trod by the gallant and true;
High, high are their hopes, for their chieftain has said,
That whatever men dare they can do.

Chorus: I hear the pibroch sounding, etc

Oh proudly they walk, though each Cameron knows
He may tread on the heather no more;
But boldly he follows his chief to the field,
Where his laurels were gathered before.

Chorus: I hear the pibroch sounding, etc

'The March of the Cameron Men' is one of those songs that has everyone joining in the chorus, yet very few amateur singers include it in their repertoire simply because the vocal range (almost two octaves with arpeggios and 'leaps') is too challenging for most untrained voices. Love it as we may in Scotland, we have tended to sit back and enjoy the likes of Kenneth Mckellar do it justice. It seemed remarkable, then, to come across a singer in the Codroy Valley who knew it better than most folk in Scotland. But, as Jerome's neighbour, Brian Farrell, put it, "Boy! I tell you, that Jerome could sing like nobody else!"

Jerome, who introduced it as 'The Cameron Men', learned the song from his school-teacher, Miss Bruce, (as she was then). Looking back, he appreciated the fact that music was encouraged at school and they were fortunate enough to have a good teacher. Then, master of understatement, he glossed over his own part, as if every schoolboy learned to the same standard. Decades later, however, his younger brother Joe remembered this song as a sort of turning point for Jerome:

> I think he was thirteen or fourteen and he was at a concert, and Anne Bruce at that time, later Anne Martin, and she had him sing a few songs. But the one that brought him fame was 'The March of the Cameron Men'… And you'd have the likes of Duncan Jim MacIsaac and Allan MacArthur who were just astounded at his ability to sing it and the feeling he put into it… [from then on] there was such acclaim about his singing. He became an entertainer.

More than forty years later, (a testimony to true appreciation), 84 year-old Allan MacArthur took me to one of those kitchen 'times' where I first met Jerome and heard him sing. It was in the home of the long-retired school teacher, Anne Martin, her kitchen a-buzz with conversation, laughter, songs, music and dancing. Allan himself, well-known as a Gaelic singer and piper, had long been regarded as the most knowledgeable custodian of Highland tradition in the Valley. What impressed him may not have been simply that a youngster with a good voice sang an old Highland song, but rather *how* he sang it. As anyone who has ever been moved by singing will know, it is not so much the words of a song that bring a tear to the eye; it is more that indescribable quality of tone and emotion which touches the heart.

So what of the song itself? The composer was unknown when Allan's maternal grandparents left Moidart, the area adjacent to Cameron territory, but well he knew their connection to that clan, as his own people were among their loyal followers. Allan's mother, Jenny MacIsaac, was only an infant when her people had to emigrate, the ultimate 'reward' for a grandfather's response to Cameron of Locheil's call to arms in 1745. As the song was composed long after the event, however, it is sometimes relegated to an era of romanticism, particularly by the Scots at home, who forget (or don't know) that the words ring true in the context of the historical background. Yet the impact of that era continued to be felt for decades, especially by families that were cleared, such as the MacArthurs, MacIsaacs and MacNeils of the Codroy Valley.

The story behind the song is best told by Mary Maxwell Campbell[1], who composed it in 1829, but like other women of her time, did not own up to her composition till speculation began to attribute it to others: 'I composed the song when very young, after travelling from morning to night through Highland scenery, with a member of the family of Lochiel.'[2] The long journey was spent listening to one of the Camerons who had actually lived through the 'Forty-five', as the last Jacobite Rising came to be known – from the optimism of August 1746 when the loyal clan chief, Cameron of Lochiel, marched with his men from Loch Arkaig to Glenfinnan, to join Prince Charles Edward Stuart in raising the standard for King James VIII, to the end of the long, sad story, the disastrous defeat at Culloden the following April. History aside, however, the song's timelessness is in its celebration of the enduring quality of loyalty that is still attributed to Scottish regiments.[3]

Understandably, the song became popular on both sides of the Atlantic, especially at concerts and clan gatherings, usually sung by classically trained performers to piano or orchestral accompaniment. Outside that circuit, it became widely available on 78 rpm records, as early as Victor label's 1908 recording of the Canadian tenor Harold Jarvis.[4] The song was also translated into Gaelic at the turn of the twentieth century and recorded by 'concert platform' singers, such as Neil Mclean (b. 1895) who sang it at a 'Royal Command Performance'. Today, it is a favourite with leading Gaelic choirs, who sing it briskly with a rousing four-part harmony chorus.[5] It is doubtful if Jerome ever heard any of the recordings, yet the amount of feeling he puts into the song may have few equals, except perhaps in Jarvis.

---

[1] Daughter of Dugald Campbell of Skerrington, Ayrshire, Mary Maxwell Campbell also composed 'The Lament for Glencoe', which seems reason enough to conceal the Campbell name as it tells of the Campbells of Argyll who slaughtered the MacDonalds at the Massacre of Glencoe in 1698. (She refers to those Campbells as 'cruel as adders'.)

[2] *Scots Minstrelsie: A National Monument of Scottish Song*, Vol. 3, p. xxiii.

[3] The amalgamation of Scottish regiments in 2006 marked the end of an era for distinctive regiments such as the Queen's Own Cameron Highlanders (founded in 1793) and Cameronians, (founded in 1881), as they were all merged into the Royal Regiments of Scotland. Canada still retains two Cameron regiments: The Queen's Own Cameron Highlanders of Canada (founded 1910) and the Cameron Highlanders of Ottawa (founded in 1856), both of which fought in the two World Wars. Both Canadian regiments wear tartan on dress occasions.

[4] Son of the professional singer Annie McLear, Harold Jarvis was born in Toronto, and is said to have worn the kilt as a child. The recording, made in Camden, New Jersey, is part of the Library of Congress collection of historical sound recordings, now available online. http://www.loc.gov/jukebox/recordings/detail/id/1432/autoplay/true.

[5] Translated by Rev. D. MacNaughtan, it was published in *A' Choisir-chiuil: The St. Columba Collection of Gaelic Songs*, p. 21.

In recent years the tune has been adapted for the Highland bagpipe, though it does not actually fit the pipe scale. It's all a matter of taste for those who don't mind a flattened note jarring the first line of every verse. As the professional recordings all seem to have fairly strident accompaniments, it was not until I heard Jerome's *a capella* rendition, combined with his measured interpretation of the song, that I stopped to reconsider 'The March of the Cameron Men'. Surely it was never intended to be performed as a brisk march, for in reality the song is about the men who led the march for a cause that is pivotal to the history of Scotland and of the Scots overseas. Jerome's unhurried rendition reflects not only his own depth of feeling and understanding but also the sense the dignity evoked by Mary Maxwell Cameron in her memory of these loyal men.

On the Wings of a Dove

On the wings of a snow white dove
He sends His pure sweet love
A sign from above
On the wings of a dove.

When trouble surrounds us when evils come
The body grows weak and the spirit grows numb
When these things beset us He does not forget us
He sends down his love on the wings of a dove.

On the wings of a snow white dove...

When Noah had drifted on the flood many days[1]
He searched for land in various ways
Troubles he had some, but he was not forgotten
He sent down His love on the wings of a dove

On the wings of a snow white dove

'On the Wings of a Dove' was composed in the mid-1950s by the American songwriter and producer Robert B. "Bob" Ferguson (1927–2001). When country singer Ferlin Husky (b. 1926) recorded it in 1960, it became his biggest hit, topping the Country Music Charts for ten weeks and reaching number 12 on the pop charts. Reflecting on the inspiration behind his composition, Ferguson said it was simply "a personal expression of faith and joy in achieving a goal. When I wrote it, I had just completed thirteen films on wildlife, and I was elated that the job was done".[2]

---

[1] On this recording Jerome sings 'When Noah had drifted many days on the flood'.

[2] See Edward Morris, '"Wings of a Dove" Writer, Bob Ferguson, Dies at 73 in Mississippi' (2001).

As a long-time member of the local church choir, Jerome was also relied upon as a soloist. His strong, melodic voice could fill the church, long before they had electricity to power speakers. He sang with deep conviction and expression, reflecting his own faith and, for Jerome, spiritual songs were not just for church, they were (and are) for any day or location.

One of the challenges that regularly confronts solo singers is in planning a 'set' of songs, whether for an informal sing-around or a big concert. Jerome had an enviable awareness of such dynamics, no matter the occasion, and could sense the mood of the moment and recognise exactly the right time to change it. This was instinctive to him, and songs such as this became the perfect choice to release what singers recognize as lyric or melodic tension. Of equal importance to Jerome was his keen awareness of the general atmosphere among his audience as well as the social or political ambiance, which could be changed by singing a song such as this.

During this particular recording Jerome happened to miss one of the verses and so it is included here:

> When Jesus went down to the river that day
> He was baptized in the usual way
> And when it was done, God blessed his son
> He sent him his love on the wings of dove.

The Sealers' Song

On We'n'sday night, March seventeen,
our spirits mounted high
For rumour reached our Valley
that the seals were passing by.
It caused a great sensation
for it is a wondrous sight
To see those little puppy seals
in Codroy River Bight.

Some husky men from all around,
from Broad Cove to Anguille
Made ready and were outward bound
in hopes to make a kill.
Our bat and sheath-knife we must grip,
our creepers we must file
For it doesn't pay to make a slip
when running down a swile.[1]

Soon every boat was put afloat
with engines running high
It wasn't long 'fore they were out
where the seals they could espy.
Old Ambrose Reid from Woody Head
was the first man onthe ice[2]
And spurred by greed to test his speed
the seal he hit him twice.

Hynes sucked his pipe and make a swipe
that made the airways sway
But the old harp ducked between his legs
and carried him away.

---

[1] Seal. *The Dictionary of Newfoundland English* includes examples of usages, dating back to the 1600s.

[2] Woody Head was a former name for Woodville, though there are other places along the south coast named Woody Head. The name Reid is also among the settlers of that part of the Valley.

Before she reached the water's edge
Hynes managed to escape
But all hands swore she wasn't sore,
cos she hadn't got a scrape.

But when Hynes doffed his pants that night
he found to his dismay
The sly old harp had took a bite
before she made away.
Ol' Jim Hynes he made a holler
as he started for the lan'
But his mind was on the dollar
instead of the snow-pan.

As he went down he made a scream
his lungs for to relieve,
But luckily within his reach was
the husky Johnny Steve
Soon Jim resumed his tow and
he was homeward bound again,
He looked just like a Romeo
a-courting in the rain.

When Pat O'Quinn that day fell in
he suddenly was gaffed
His father missed the upper skin
but he hooked him further aft.
And after he had wrung his clothes
and stood to let them drip
His father slipped and in he goes
a-floundering in the deep.

Pat heard a scream, turned his eyes
and tried to grab his hair
But soon he was to realise
there wasn't any there.
Ryan hunted for a breeding patch
to test the federal law
But no ideas could he grasp
from anything he saw.

Is it where the old harps match and mate,
and does it move around?
Will you find it near the seaway gate
where other seals abound?
We'll ask our friend Judge Spracklin

21. The Sealers' Song

for he has a legal mind,
I'm sure he'll have that term erased
or otherwise defined.

When Duncan Jim set out to swim
his face was turning solemn,
But he worked his feet to a faster beat
to the tune of the 'Gille Calum'[3]
With his seals in tow, that man could go,
though his boots were filled with water
But neither slob nor slush, slowed
his onward rush, and he landed like an otter

Alas, sad news this sport to spoil,
from law-men, did you hear?
You must not bat a puppy swile
in the springtime of the year.
Shall we bat them in the summer-time
or bat them in the fall?
Must we join a band as drummers
if we want to bat at all?

Must we form a Sealers' Club, me boys,
to claim our share of pelts?
Or worldly wise indulge in lies
to avoid the law-man's welts?
Has freedom's flag been trampled down,
has liberty been slain?
For we may no longer earn a crown[4]
to lessen hunger's pain.

March was always long and awful,
boys, the pork barrel bottom bare,
That's when taking seals was lawful,
now the puppies must be spared.
Why, I'm sure some day a demagogue
will write up in a book
The proper way to stun a cod
before he takes the hook.

---

[3] The image conjured up by this line is very amusing, as the tune 'Gille Calum' is very popular among step-dancers in the Valley and Cape Breton, and is also played for the sword dance, performed by Highland dancers the world over. Duncan Jim MacIsaac, a Gaelic-speaker, was also Hughie's brother-in-law.

[4] A crown was five shillings, in today's terms, 25 pence. (20 shillings = £1)

An old Scottish anecdote tells of the Edinburgh butler who interrupted an afternoon tea-party to announce the invention of gaslights and the end to lighting whale-oil lamps. "What about the poor whales?" was the response that apparently dates animal rights logic to the mid-nineteenth century. There were still whaling stations in Newfoundland during the late 1960s, when, as 'poor students', we bought whale meat in the supermarkets. Whale fishery aside, however, there may no animal issue in the world more controversial (or internationally misunderstood) than Newfoundland's seal-hunt. From the early 1700s it had been built into the seasonal cycle of work and was an integral part of the way of life.[5] Whether it took place far from shore, on dangerous ice-floes with a steam-ship as the headquarters, or from land-based quarters, the seal-hunt was not only crucial to Newfoundland's economy but to sustaining families who would otherwise have died of hunger during the harsh winters.[6]

In the 1970s, however, all that was to change, thanks to the success of a worldwide campaign to persuade the public to think from the point of view of a seal. There was apparently no case for considering the viewpoint of a cod, even although he – it – along with a dozen of his kin-fish, would be eaten daily by one single seal. That species would multiply and flourish, but soon there would be no codfish left, leaving the poor seals to search for some other edible creature to sustain them. As is the way of the single-minded zealot, there would be no case for considering the Newfoundland fisherman whose livelihood would be destroyed when there was no cod left. And so, the seal-hunt, as Jerome's generation knew it, is now a thing of the past. So is the cod-fishery.[7]

---

[5] See, *The Ice Hunters: A History of Newfoundland Sealing to 1914*, by folklorist and historian Shannon Ryan, who was born and brought up among fishermen and seal-hunters.

[6] In parts of the Outer Hebrides of Scotland seal meat was eaten during Lent to supplement the diet. The subject on whether it is fish, which is 'allowed' or meat, which is 'not allowed', is discussed by Martin Martin from the Isle of Skye, after he visited South Uist during Lent in the late 1600s. See Martin Martin. *A Description of the Western Isles of Scotland circa 1695*, pp. 64–66. More than three centuries later, when wishing to find out the current attitude, I asked Canon Angus MacQueen from South Uist, an authority on both Gaelic and church doctrines. Canon MacQueen informed me that not only did the Catholic Church permit seal to be eaten during Lent, but also the cormorant may also be included in the diet. (Noted during conversation, 2001). Seal oil is still valued as a source of Omega oils, and in older Scottish tradition seal was also used as in remedy for sciatica. (The sufferer wore a tight belt of sealskin, next to the skin.) Other uses in the Hebrides included the making of strong ropes, such as those needed for fixing the plough.

[7] Newfoundland still has a seal-hunt and a fragile cod-fishing industry, conducted under new regulations, and, for the time being, protestors have a much lower profile than they once had. Newfoundlanders are, however, doing their best to hold on to their age-old tradition of seal-hunting, as a boutique selling seal-skin clothing, footwear and other products recently opened in St John's. See, *The Telegraph*, St. John's, June 13, 2012.

The hunt was notoriously dangerous, with a history of disaster and loss of life, at its worst in 1914 when 252 sealers died in horrific conditions that separated them from their ships.[8] While nobody forgets the risk, yet the hunt was anxiously anticipated every year as it was the main source of income and food for many families. Contrary to anti-sealing propaganda, seal-meat was eaten not only by hunters and their families but also by folk who had no involvement whatsoever in the catch. Living in St. John's in the late 1960s, I recall the buzz and excitement that followed radio and television announcements of (named) vessels returning from the ice. First, it was the family with whom I boarded, then it seemed as if everybody in town, headed for the waterfront, not for any spectacle but to buy seal-flippers. This was not an experience to be missed by the granddaughter of a crofter-fisherman such as I; nor was the ensuing dinner of flipper pie.

The men who had been 'out on the ice' for several weeks returned weather-beaten and unshaven, smiling, thankful to be home, 'a few dollars' in their pockets, ready for the next stage of the season's labour. Any questions I may have had about eating seal-meat (only the flippers?) were soon answered on a visit 'home' with a fellow student from an outport fishing family – early in the morning I watched the men set out a dory and return with a seal. The pelt was laid aside to be sold, then every part of it was butchered for meat. What didn't feed us that weekend was packaged and frozen, or bottled to be kept for the time of year, (usually March), when, as the song has it, the 'the pork barrel bottom [would be] bare'.[9]

Songs about the seal hunt are plentiful, all borne out of experience or the re-telling of it. Alas, too many are about tragedy and disaster, yet these songs keep alive the memories as they continue to be sung decades after the event.[10] A much happier one, 'The Sealers' Song', may be the best known, thanks to the late John White who sang it, up-tempo, to the tune of 'The Girl I left Behind Me'. It begins with a welcome celebration of the seal-hunters' safe return and concludes with 'So here's success to Susie Bess and girls from all out harbours / For a kiss set in on a sealer's chin which never saw the barber.'[11] The song was a favourite on radio and

---

[8] The account of two simultaneous ice disasters involving the SS *Newfoundland* and the SS *Southern Cross*, was recorded by Cassie Brown in her book, *Death on the Ice; The Great Newfoundland Sealing Disaster of 1914*. See also John Scott, " 'I Don't Think There's Anything in the World That the Common Man Will Take a Bigger Chance [For] Than He'll Take For a Seal'.

[9] In the Codroy Valley, Allan MacArthur's wife Mary described how they used to bottle meat to keep it for the winter, see, *The Last Stronghold*, pp. 94–96.

[10] Paul Mercer lists a dozen songs about the seal hunt in his book, *Newfoundland Songs and Ballads in Print, 1842–1974*, see p. 174. This song is not among them.

[11] As the main singer of a popular CBC television series, 'All Around the Circle', (1964 to 1975), the late John White was the weekly entertainment in every home

television and every household had a copy of the words, since they were printed in a free booklet, *Songs Of Newfoundland,* distributed all over the province.¹²

Regarding the episode that inspired the song, Jerome added that it was not particularly common for seals to go ashore near the mouth of the Grand Codroy River – he hadn't seen them since 1965, the episode that occasioned Hughie O'Quinn's song. As he explained:

> They weren't sealers, they were just landsmen and a lot of them fell in .... And they almost lost two or three but they all got ashore. And this Jim Hynes, he's in the song, said, "Hughie, you should make a song." And the next morning Hughie handed in the song...¹³

While Hughie O'Quinn's composition is also light-hearted, it has the stamp of the satirist on it, as he makes playful jest of the sealers and their ploys before firing a squib at the controversy surrounding the hunt. While the song is instantly identifiable as local (Codroy River Bight), by the second verse 'Broad Cove to Anguille' there's a sense of a much wider geographic reach than any of Hughie's other songs. Nevertheless, the listener must wait to discover whether this is of any significance or not. As the style is reminiscent of a 'Come-all-ye', the anticipated 'take warning by me' advice follows an amusing, if unfortunate, incident: "It doesn't pay to make a slip when running down a swile".

It is acceptable in this tradition to make fun of misadventure, provided the only hurt inflicted is to personal pride, and not to body or soul. It may be the choice of tune however – the rebel song 'The Wearing of the Green'¹⁴ – that hints at O'Quinn's real purpose: to have a go at the political

---

in Newfoundland and Labrador. An all-time favourite voice on radio and records, he helped popularize many songs, especially those with a Newfoundland-Irish flavour.

¹² *Op. Cit. pp. 9–11.*

¹³ MUNFLA 88-226

¹⁴ To anyone familiar with the words of the song, even the tune evokes protest, as it dates back to the 1798 Irish Rebellion when there was outrage at the banning of symbols such as the shamrock, which displayed loyalty to Ireland. As the seal-hunt is part of Newfoundland's identity, we get the gist, even from one verse of the old song: "Oh. Paddy dear and did you hear the news that's going round?/The shamrock is by law forbid to grow on Irish ground./St. Patrick's Day no more we'll keep, his colour can't be seen/ For they're hanging men and women for the wearing of the green." And, lest the historical facts be doubted, in singing the song Dominic Behan summed up the situation as "Another little trick of Mother England's, imprison a man for respecting his country's National Emblems. Dispossess him if he used the Irish form of his name. Hang him if he objected." See *Ireland Sings,* note to song number 96.

rumblings that were erupting at the time. With the skill of the satirist he succeeds, waiting till verses 11 and 12 before considering the extent to which some people will go to test the law. He poses a string of questions, which, to the fisherman or hunter, may be so absurd that they scarcely merit response. On their behalf, O'Quinn fires the final rocket, well crafted and accurately aimed:

> I'm sure some day a demagogue will write up in a book
> The proper way to stun a cod before he takes the hook.

While it may seem pedantic to quote the *Oxford English Dictionary* definition of demagogue – 'a political leader who seeks support by appealing to popular desires and prejudices rather than by using rational argument' – it serves to affirm the song-maker's precision in hitting his target. When the letter of the law triumphs over feeding the hungry, then logic is turned on its head. Meanwhile the fisherman is left to consider the ludicrous proposal – picture this – of doing everything backwards: bait the hooks, cast the lines, land the catch, stun the fish, remove the hooks – in reverse order. A demonstration is called for, in both senses of the word.

If it takes some attention to catch the innuendo in O'Quinn's song, it takes even more (not to mention skill) to learn the song and sing it, especially when there is no manuscript or printed page at hand. Such was the impact of the song on Jerome that he could sing it after hearing it only once, 'putting it together to the tune' as he pictured the local men involved.

As he also followed the local and the national news, Jerome was well aware of the political and economic context of Hughie's song. Such subjects were, and still are, the day-to-day conversation of a people concerned about political decisions that affect communities. It is not the politician's speech that keeps social, moral or legal matters in the public consciousness, however, as there will be other speeches tomorrow that will dim today's. But, if a song is composed about a controversy, therein lies power to keep the issue alive; and as long as there is someone who cares enough to sing the song, then concerns such as those for the fishing industry, or the livelihood of fishermen, will not be allowed to die.

Winnie MacNeil

George O'Quinn from Grand River Millville do reside,
Goes courting a lassie from this other side.
Goes courting a lassie, her name I'll reveal,
The name of this lassie is Winnie MacNeil.

He'll go down to Angus's, there sit and talk,
Then he and his Winnie goes out for a walk.
And when he gets out, then how glad he will feel,
Oh, Winnie, oh Winnie, oh Winnie MacNeil.

On the football field, sure he's one of the boys.
When Winnie is watching how hard he will try
To be the best player that's on the field,
Oh, Winnie, oh Winnie, oh Winnie MacNeil.

If he chances to meet you upon the main road,
First thing he will ask you if you got your horse shod.
And if you have not, then the next thing he'll do
Is tell you of Angus and how he can shoe.[1]

He'll go over to Wallace Ben's, now sits a while,
And to keep him busy it is quite a trial.
And late in the evening there's lumber to scale,
Oh, Winnie, oh Winnie, oh Winnie MacNeil.

On this cold December nothing to amuse,
But set in a corner and play with her shoes.
I can't tell the creature how lonely I feel,
Oh, Winnie, oh, Winnie, oh, Winnie MacNeil.

---

[1] By 2012 I did not encounter anyone, even among the elderly, who remembered a blacksmith or smithy on that stretch of the road. Nevertheless, a note in the local newspaper of 1904 stated that: "Angus MacNeil, Grand River, opened a blacksmiths' shop at Pushthrough." *The Western Star*, Cornerbrooke, June 29, 1904. (Fieldwork notes, 1968.)

Oh there's more of his troubles that now I will list,
On a cold frosty morning the engine will miss –
And George's lips parched for the want of a kiss.
Tis this very evening away I will steal –
Oh, Winnie, oh Winnie, oh Winnie MacNeil.

When he met with his Winnie so handsome and sweet,
He kissed her so often on both of the cheeks,
He was spitting powder the rest of that week –
Oh, Winnie, oh Winnie, oh Winnie, how sweet!

Oh the time it is come, I think I might say,
For us to appoint our wedding day.
I think we'll appoint it down in John Dan's hay.
I don't mean the hay that's surrounding the field –
Oh, Winnie, oh Winnie, oh Winnie MacNeil.

Now to conclude and to finish my song,
If you'll pay attention it won't take me long.
All that I wish you is one million cheers,
And hope you live happy for ten thousand years.

In the early 1930s, when Paulie Hall composed this song, he was in his mid-thirties and lived alone in the cabin, which was to be his home for the rest of his life. He was to remain a bachelor and, even into old age, lived up to his reputation of being fascinated by the subjects of courtship and marriage. Karen (Cormier) Farrell, who was only thirteen when she accompanied me on a visit, recalls the first question he asked us was, "Are you girls married?" (The other 'girls' were 23 and 15.)

From his house on the top of the hill Paulie enjoyed watching, or hearing about, all the comings and goings of the Valley. He welcomed friends and neighbours who stopped by, and at times when he was hired by folk who needed a hand, he enjoyed the chance to sit in someone else's kitchen, sharing company, food, news and songs. As a young man, Jerome had occasionally worked alongside Paul, though later in life, most of the visits they spent were in Paul's bachelor cabin in Millville: "Some of the boys would gather for a few songs, maybe a game of cards and a jar of home-brew."

In a discussion on how he chose the subjects for his songs, Paul explained to John Szwed that, local 'news' he didn't see for himself might still be supplied when, as he put it, "some of the young fellas would come around and give me the pointers about people" – 'pointers' being the gossip that occasioned the composition of such a song.² Though Paul himself enjoyed teasing young folk through his songs, there is also the implication that 'the young fellas' found in Paul an ideal means to stirring up embarrassment while they stood back and laughed at other people's expense (including Paul's). As far as Paul was concerned, there would be no telling who would be next: "And sometimes I'd turn it around and made one on them that gave me the facts, so that they'd be more careful the next time."³ When he told us 'girls' that he was 'soon going to make some now about the young ones courting'⁴ he gave no hint of how serious he was, but gave the impression that all it would take would be some 'pointer' and, to use Brian Farrell's expression, Paul would be off "like a herd of turtles'.

The 'young ones' immortalized in his songs may have been equally unaware of the bard's intentions, as George O'Quinn was about seventeen at the time, and Winnie a year or two younger. George was the eldest son of the family who lived next-door, and though he had known Paul all his life, he was probably unaware that even the direction he walked across the adjacent field could be observed and noted by the local satirist. Meanwhile, Winnie lived across the river in Upper Ferry, which Paul called 'Scotchytown', about half a mile from the bridge that opened when she was only eight years old.

Martin MacArthur (b. 1926), who was eight years younger than Winnie, explained that from the late 1920s it was the custom "for boys and girls them days to walk down to the bridge, because round about the cross-roads and over near the bridge used to be the meeting place..." He laughed as he recalled how "a bunch of them would come over from Great Codroy, O'Regans and Millville.... and one time Paulie Hall made a song about them."⁵ Without hesitation, his brother Sears (b. 1934) responded by quoting the entire first verse:

> George O'Quinn from Grand River Millville did reside,
> Went courting a lassie from the other side...

Like all the older generation, the MacArthur brothers knew the road to the bridge like the back of their hands, as Sears said:

> It was three miles from the old Searston church up near the Gut (the mouth of the Grand Codroy River) to the Loch Lomond cross roads [where Winnie lived, and 200 yards from the MacArthurs' home]. Then another mile from this cross roads to the Upper

---

² Szwed, Op cit. p. 155.

³ *Op cit.* p. 155

⁴ Recorded in Paul's cabin, July 1970, MUNFLA C871-71-48

⁵ Martin and his brother Sears were recorded in Upper Ferry on June 17, 2012.

Ferry cross roads. And from there to the other side of the bridge, less than a mile.

As Martin and Sears were related by marriage to Winnie MacNeil, I asked them if they thought she might have been embarrassed by the song. In unison they replied, "Oh, I think she would have been." But, as Martin added:

> That was what they used to do in those days, making up verses... and like everyone else, you'd get over it... Then Winnie went away to Cape Breton to work, like our sister Margaret. A lot of the girls from the Valley went over to work there, same as some of the men went to work in the coal-mine, the girls went over to do house-work. And Winnie met this man, and they moved to St. Catherine's when they got married over there. And she never came home....Oh, they're both gone now... that's a long time ago. But Jerome Downey, he could sing you the song...

The Thomas Cat

Did you ever hear the story about the Thomas cat?
He is a noble animal, he lives on mutton fat;
He is a noble animal, he is so cute and sly,
He whacks his paw into the bowl and he makes the gravy fly.

He is a noble animal, his head is full of sense,
When he wants to meet his Miss he goes upon the fence,
Saying, 'Oh Pussycat, where have you been at?'
You've been off keeping comp'ny with some other Thomas cat?

The cats they have a concert at the end of every year
And the way they began it is gnawing on their ear,
First they began to hawk and squawk and then they make *Miaow*!
Back upon their muzzle and the fur begins to fly.

This light-hearted song was one that goes back to Jerome's childhood when he heard it from a neighbour, who was contemporary of their grandfather's: "Tom Cornelly – he died in 1960 at a hundred years old." The name turns up in local records as 'Corneally' but Jerome and his family pronounced it 'Cornelly' and, as can be seen from MacEdward Leach in 1951, that is also how the man himself said it.[1] Jerome's brother Joe, who was familiar with him, both as a neighbour and via local history research, noted: "His name was used as Cornelly in the Valley but on the census and on a deed for land it is listed as Corneally."[2] The family originally came from Nova Scotia and in Grand Codroy around 1900, not far from the Downeys – the Newfoundland Census for 1921 has both families listed in the entry for Great Codroy (St. Georges District).[3] Before the

---

[1] http://www.mun.ca/folklore/leach/songs/index.html. 'The Thomas Cat' sung by Tom Cornelly MUNFLA 78-054 NFLD2, Tape 23, track 5.

[2] Personal correspondence, Joe Downey, 2012.

[3] Tom Cornelly (with yet another spelling, possibly an error in copying so, to avoid further confusion, it is not noted here) and his extended family are listed at Dwelling Number 27. The Downey family is listed at Dwelling Number 14 (not to be confused with two other Downey families at numbers 21 and 24).

bridge across the Grand Codroy River was built in 1923, Tom operated a ferry-boat across the river to Upper Ferry. Although the ferry ceased operation before Jerome was born, the settlement still retains its name.

Nothing seems to be known about the origins of the song, though perhaps Mr. Cornelly may have known, since the only version of it that appears in an archive catalogue is one that he himself sang in 1951 for a visiting American folklorist. The tune is remarkably close to a macaronic song, 'MacDonald's First Visit to Glasgow', recorded in the 1930s by Scottish Gaelic singer Archie Grant, and as popular in Nova Scotia as in Scotland.[4] While the song itself may not seem to be of much significance, in the context of singers as well as the collectors from two (if not three) generations, it turns up interesting information. Professor MacEdward Leach (1897–1967), who recorded Tom Cornelly, was founder of the Folklore Department at the University of Pennsylvania, where Kenny Goldstein (1933–2000), who recorded this collection, was one of his students.[5]

In two fieldtrips to Newfoundland during the summers of 1950 and 1951, Leach recorded over 600 songs and, as his fieldwork notes show, the last tape he recorded was of Tom Cornelly.[6] The titles of nine songs are listed, but, uncharacteristically, Leach did not write down the name of the place where the tape was recorded, (folklorists sometimes get tired). As it was made at the very end of his trip, however, it was probably during one of several stops on his long journey home.[7]

As part of the 'MacEdward Leach Newfoundland Collection' now in the Memorial University of Newfoundland Folklore Archive, the reel-to-reel tapes have been digitized and songs can be heard on-line.[8] Apart from satisfying the interest in hearing the voice of Tom Cornelly, by then aged 90, obtaining access to both recordings presents a unique opportunity of

---

[4] The Beltona recording (BL.4031-B Matrix M.866), now out of copyright, may be heard on , http://archive.org/details/raretunes_230_macdonalds-first-visit-glasgow.

[5] Kenny later became a colleague, and then Director. The influence of these two folklorists is immeasurable in the world of folklore scholarship.

[6] The University of Pennsylvania Folklore Archive listing is: 'Leach Newfoundland Collection.' Tom Cornelly. Newfoundland. Reel to reel, sound recording, 1951. T-82-00007-79, 79.

[7] A car journey from the Avalon Peninsula to the ferry at Port aux Basques would not have been made in one day before the existence of the Trans-Canada Highway. It may well have taken several days, as MacEdward Leach's 1950 fieldtrip concludes with west coast stops at Curling, Port aux Port, Flat Rock and Cape Ray, where he recorded the last tapes of his 1950 collection, numbered 29-37. Following a similar pattern in 1951, it is most likely that he recorded his very last tape, involving Tom Cornelly, *after* he had crossed the ferry to Nova Scotia, as Jerome's brother Joe, who remembers the family well, explained that, Mr Cornelly returned to Nova Scotia in 1942. (Personal correspondence, Joe Downey, 2012)

[8] http://www.mun.ca/folklore/leach/songs/index.html.

comparing the 'learned version' (Jerome's) with that of the 'source singer' (Tom Cornelly). This is an exciting prospect for anyone interested in the process of learning, as well as for folklorists, ever fascinated by the world of oral transmission. Apart from Jerome's surprise 'Miaow', reflecting his sense of fun, and three words (hop, hawk; biting, gnawing; and muscle, muzzle, which may be discrepancies in transcription or Jerome's interpretation[9]), he sings exactly the same three verses, word for word. Not only does Jerome sing precisely the same tune, but also, despite the years between recordings, he sings it in the same key!

---

[9] In the first instance, 'hawk' creates the internal rhyme, which is natural to Irish singers, and, having a longer vowel than 'hop', it also fits the tune better. In the second instance, where Jerome clearly enunciates a 'z', the word 'muzzle' may have made more sense to a man so familiar with animals. Jerome would refer to the facial area of a cat or dog as the 'muzzle' and, since this amusing drama began with a bite on the ear, this may be the implication.

Micky Jim MacNeil

Oh, I worked up in Scotchytown,
I liked my work and master fine,
We usually make hay
when the sun so bright do shine.
We usually went to it
till the sun you couldn't see –
I like them old-time Scotchmen,
for they make the good strong tea.

Here I'm up in Scotchytown,
I hope I brought a cheer,
Mr Angus MacIsaac is
the oldest Scotchman here.
He's getting old and feeble,
his locks are turning grey –
I like that old-time Scotchman,
for he makes the good strong tea.

Mr A.D. MacIsaac owns
a large grocery store –
No other in the Valley
so good to help the poor.
Whatever you will ask of him,
his kind heart will agree.
I like that old-time Scotchman,
for he makes the good strong tea.

You'll hear jokes on the Scotchman
from morning, noon, till night,
And when you chance to hear them,
they'll always say they're tight.
But I'll give you my opinion,
well I'll tell you how I feel,

The tightest of the Scotchmen
was this Micky Jim MacNeil.

As he strolled down one evening
to cross Grand River wide,
Little thinking of the danger
that lies within its tide,
The ice that he was walking on
gave way beneath his pins,
There was nothing for the Scotchman
but to go in to the chin.

When he hit the cold water,
so loudly did he roar,
Two men went to his rescue
from the old churchyard shore.
One man says to the other,
before we launch a boat,
We'll have to try to find out
if they put him in to soak.

But while the men were talking,
he made another roar,
They quickly launched a dory
and they brought him safe to shore,
He said, "I'm going to tell you,
as soon as I get dry,
I'll never more go on the ice
without a stick to try."

The time of his misfortune,
was in the early spring,
Many's the good old Scotchman's friend
got soaked right to the skin,
When he got back to shore again,
the ones he hadn't lost
All had a better appetite
when Micky had a wash.

Come, Micky, pay attention,
and voice to you I'll send,
What worse crime did you e'er commit
than to drown your bosom friend?

> When you're walking on the ice,
> oh don't you be so bold,
> Remember that in wintertime
> the water it is cold!

Jerome began by saying, "This song is 'Micky Jim MacNeil' by Paulie Hall... he made it in the early Thirties." Having heard the song when he was very young, Jerome also knew all the people mentioned, who were all "from the other side of the river". With his parents, brothers and sisters he had walked past their houses twice every Sunday on the way to church and back. As anyone of his generation recalls, everyone went to mass on Sunday and all through Lent, then on Christmas Eve the whole church would be packed. Besides that, you could walk through the door of any of them when you'd be out mummering.[1]

The song begins with the best of Paul's experience of 'Scotchytown', which is the name he gives to the settlement now known as Upper Ferry. According to Mrs Allan (Mary) MacArthur it was formerly known as MacDale, and kept that name until a little post office closed.[2] As Paul pays affectionate tribute to several of the older folk, the first-time listener does not suspect that the bard is about to sharpen his focus (as well as his tongue) and fix on one man, Micky Jim MacNeil. Since, from all accounts, Micky was a mild-mannered, well-liked individual, we might wonder why Paul unleashes his pen in this fashion? But, as two of his nephews, Martin and Sears MacArthur recalled, "This was pay-back time. Micky had made a song about Paulie – it was something about his horse, and the harness on his horse and Paul wouldn't like that. So now it was his turn to get his own back."[3]

Martin also had vivid memories of the incident that gave Paul his chance to compose his most scathing satire:

> Micky was manager of the Co-op up at Upper Ferry and part of his job was that he'd go around from farm to farm and he'd get orders for mutton, and maybe beef, to sell at the Co-op. And this time he left from his home up on the hill there, and walked across to Mike Tom Downey's on the north side there, the old man, for orders. And he walked across the river there where he shouldn't have, though the river was frozen, and what happened, but he fell through the ice. And they had an awful job to get him. Mike

---

[1] See, *The Last Stronghold*, pp. 100 –117.

[2] *Ibid*, p. 62.

[3] Summarised from the conversation with Martin and Sears recorded in Sears MacArthur's home, Upper ferry, June 26, 2012.

Tom and his son Hyacinth had a boat – and this was in the wintertime. And myself and Dad, we were at the wood-pile at the time, and we heard the commotion – we could hear something going on over there. And this is what it was – they were trying to rescue Micky. So, they got out so far, and they had to be careful too in case they got into trouble. And Micky was just about gone when they got him onto the ice. And they got him home, and he was up at Mike Tom Downey's for, oh I forget how long, but I think it was weeks instead of days. And Mike Tom Downey's wife, she was a, not a full-fledged nurse, but she had, what they say, nursing knowledge. But I would think that that was something that may have caused Micky's illness and early death, he got such a chill. They just got him in time. I wasn't very old at the time, but oh, I remember it, yes, yes.

There is no hint of this crisis when Paul's song begins, but as the verses unfold he has a field-day satirising his fellow song-maker, testing his mettle in every verse. If his aim was to let a fellow bard know what it felt like to be on the receiving end of a satire, Paul undoubtedly succeeded. He contrasts the kindness of 'the old-time Scotchmen' with Micky, whom he calls 'tight', that most disliked of terms among Scots the world over. In withholding the information that Micky was employed by the local Co-operative store to buy and sell produce on behalf of local farmers, offering a fair deal for all, Paul personalises the transactions for maximum effect. But that is merely the platform from which to fire his remaining missiles.

Short of calling Micky lousy (a condition well known to Paul from the lumber-camp bunkhouses), he doesn't hold back, suggesting that Micky may even have been 'put in to soak' (never mind the fact that he almost died). Finally, adding insult to injury, he accuses Micky of drowning his 'bosom friends'.

In his article 'Paul E. Hall: A Newfoundland Song-Maker And His Community', John Szwed writes that 'the satirical songmaker walks the thin line between amusement and libel.' Yet, as far as we know, it was all taken in good sport. Aside from testing the character of the other bard – 'If you dish it out, you might have to take it' – there is much more to the song than just 'having a dig'. Years on, it becomes a social document recording who's who in the community. As soon as Jerome finished the song, anticipating a question, he continued the conversation:

Jerome: Now Angus MacIsaac was a real old man, they used to call him 'Angus hardwood'.[4] Do you know Duncan Jim MacLellan? (The one that fell in the water in Hughie O'Quinn's 'Sealer's Song'.) Well, he was his grandfather! [laughs]

---

[4] According to the 1921 Census he was born in Scotland in 1844.

KG: And who was Micky Jim MacNeil?

Jerome: Now, you know Hughie MacNeil, who lived over there?[5] Now, that was – well, I'll tell you – Allan MacArthur was married to his sister [Cecilia MacNeil] But other than that, he goes way back.

MB: That was Allan's first wife, Frank's mother – she died just after Loretta was born... [aside to Kenny, *We're going to visit Frank – he's the one who sings Gaelic songs.*]

Jerome: His first wife, yes... you know more about this than I do, I believe!

MB: Oh, no, I just know the family...

Had there been a kitchen full of local folk, the conversation may well have taken off, as, time and time again, discussions about family connections and the Valley itself continue to be an important part of getting together.

Not only people are remembered, but also landmarks: particularly the Searston Church, which once drew folk together on a daily basis. Beautifully and skilfully constructed by the early settlers, it held an imposing position towards the mouth of the Grand Codroy River. It could be seen far out to sea, as well as from both sides of the river, right down to O'Regans, beyond where the Downey's lived. Torn down in the Seventies, and replaced by a modern church two miles inland, its removal seems to have left bigger scars on the community than on the landscape, which has been smoothed over.

The unpaved road that Jerome and his brothers walked all those years ago may now have changed beyond recognition. Yet it is neither in the improved road, nor in the construction of new, fancy houses nor even in the appearance of huge satellite dishes that the greatest changes are felt. In fact, without a doubt, some of these alterations have been welcomed, and, for most folk, there is still a vibrant sense of community. It is more in the intangible aspects that Jerome's generation feel a sense of loss, as they reflect on their contentment with fewer material possessions and the unquestioned depth of faith that once was at the heart of every family.

As for Micky Jim MacNeil and the other folk in the song and conversation, they represent just a few of the Gaelic speakers numbered in the Grand River census of 1921. Along that stretch of road from Searston Church past the MacArthurs, MacNeils and MacIsaacs mentioned, there were nearly two hundred Gaelic speakers when Paulie Hall was young. Today there are only two left in the Valley:[6] Allan and Mary MacArthur's son, Sears, and his sister Margaret (Cormier), in whose homes there is still a Gaelic 'presence' regularly kept alive through music and songs, as well as occasional conversations with visitors from Cape Breton or Scotland.

---

[5] Younger brother of Winnie, of the Paul Hall's song.

[6] There are two more brothers from the MacArthur family: Dan, who lives in Cape Breton and Martin who lives in Alberta.

Today

Today, while the blossoms still cling to the vine
I'll taste your strawberries, I'll drink your sweet wine.
A million tomorrows will all pass away
Ere I forget all the joy that is mine, today

I'll be a rover, and I'll be a dandy
You'll know who I am by the songs that I sing.
I'll feast at your table, I'll sleep in your clover
Who cares what tomorrow shall bring?

Today, while the blossoms still cling to the vine...

I can't be contented with yesterday's glory
I can't live on promises winter to spring.
Today is my moment, and now is my story
I'll laugh and I'll cry and I'll sing.

Today, while the blossoms still cling to the vine...

This song was originally composed as part of the sound-track of a Hollywood movie, 'Advance to the Rear' (1964), set at the time of the American Civil War (1861–1865). Though the plot was fictional, the songs woven through it are sometimes assumed to be folksongs from that era. Composer of the sound-track was singer-songwriter Randy Sparks, who also founded The New Christy Minstrels. Although this group sang backing tracks in the film, with Sparks as lead singer, they are much more famous for their live performances, televisions series and records. Anyone in Canada with a radio or television in the Sixties or Seventies could scarcely have missed them, as they were darlings of their day: ten fresh, young faces, perfect smiles, effortless performances and polished arrangements as well as matching suits and dresses with starched petticoats. The group appeared on CBC television stations all across the country, though their popularity in Newfoundland, however, was more from air-play on country music radio stations and local juke-boxes – a common feature of 'diners' and roadside restaurants.

As there are many 'cover' versions of the song, the most famous being John Denver's 1974 recording, its route to the Downey's fireside is not easy to identify. Jerome simply liked the song and, given the speed at which he learned new songs, when he heard one that appealed to him, it soon became part of his repertoire. Stripped of all the backing tracks, 'Today' becomes Jerome's song, with only one slight change to the text: 'the morrow' (line 8) is replaced with 'tomorrow', more in keeping with the local mode of expression. Interestingly, Jerome's melody to this deceptively simple song is much closer to the original composed by Randy Sparks than that recorded by John Denver – in all but the final chorus, Denver simplifies the third line, singing the same note on all five syllables of 'million tomorrows'. More important here than analysing the minutiae of composition, however, is the ability to relate to the interpretation by the singer – in Jerome's case, every time he sang it he conveyed part of his own philosophy of life: he was truly contented with his surroundings and the joy of sharing his songs.

The Wee Cooper o' Fife

There was a wee cooper who lived in Fife
 Nickety, nackety, noo, noo, noo
And he has gotten a gentle wife
 Hey Willie Wallacky, hey John Dougall
 Alane quo' Rushety, roue, roue, roue.

She wouldna bake, she wouldna brew
 Nickety, nackety, noo, noo, noo
For spoiling o' her comely hue
 Hey Willie Wallacky, hey John Dougall
 Alane quo' Rushety, roue, roue, roue.

She wouldna wash, she wouldna wring,
For spoiling o' her gowden ring

She wouldna caird, she wouldna spin
For shaming o' her gentle kin

The cooper has gone to his wool shack
And laid a sheepskin on his wife's back

Oh, I'll no' thrash ye for your kin
But I will thrash my ain sheepskin

Oh, I will bake and I will brew
And think nae mair o' my comely hue

Oh, I will wash and I will wring
And think nae mair o' my gowden ring

I will caird and I will spin
And think nae mair o' my gentle kin

Noo ye that hae gotten a gentle wife
Just think ye on the wee cooper of Fife

There can be few field-working folklorists who have not run out of tape or suddenly found that the batteries failed, putting an abrupt end to a recording session. Perhaps the general expectation may be that a fragment such as this should be relegated to the cutting floor with 'left-over scraps' (of which there are several). Nevertheless, it is included in this collection partly because it is the only Classic Ballad recorded from Jerome's repertoire.

A variant of 'The Wife Wrapt in Wether's Skin' (Child number 277)[1], it is known in Scotland as 'The Wee Cooper of Fife'. Without the complete recording of Jerome's singing is not now possible to know which verses he sang; but I have placed the fragment as verse 2 within the most commonly sung verses.[2] It is not so much for the text as for the tune that it is included here, however, as Jerome sings a catchy and unusual variant, a little gem, which I had not come across elsewhere.

---

[1] Francis James Child, *The English and Scottish Popular Ballads*, Vol. V, pp.104–107. Roud 117.

[2] The song was known all over Scotland as it was widely taught in schools. American singer Burl Ives recorded the song, sung to the commonly used tune, http://www.raretunes.org/recordings/wee-cooper-o-fife/. It was also printed in the *Family Herald & Weekly Star* .

AFTERWORD

It may seem redundant, if not careless, to have two tracks of the same song ('On the Wings of a Dove'), sung by the same singer on the one CD. It is not due to any oversight, however, that recordings made in 1980 and 2007 are both included, but rather as a testimony to Jerome's musicality and the vital role of songs in his life. After more than eighty years of singing, Jerome's world changed considerably when illness intervened and he could no longer set off with Rosie for a ceilidh or get-together. Giving up the church choir must have felt like the last straw to him as he faced his diagnosis of Alzheimer's disease. Meanwhile, the close-knit community also had to accept that, after all those years of sharing social and church events, they could no longer have the pleasure of Jerome's company or his singing. Confined to home, he gradually became more withdrawn as he adapted to declining health.

In 2007, having planned to visit Jerome and Rosie after many years of not seeing them, I was dismayed to hear of his illness and filled with disbelief at being told he no longer sang. To a singer, life without songs is unthinkable, yet it was the friendship, valued far above all the songs that motivated my visit – I would be content simply sitting in silence. In any case, I told myself, why should he remember me, as it had been years since I had been over his doorstep? (At this point, now as then, I hear folk say they scarcely remember names of folk they met last week.) And so, off we set.

One of the most emotive moments of any 'fieldwork' I have ever done, was when Jerome turned from gazing vacantly out of the window, looked directly at me and said, "I knows you!" His face shone with recognition as he added, "We used to sing!" The trigger was not a song, but the sound of my speaking voice – within minutes of hearing it, Jerome was completely engaged. To see him light up, laugh, converse, sing and play his fiddle and accordion on that afternoon would remain imprinted in my memory, had the microphone been left behind.

At the age of 84, not only could Jerome sing melodiously and remember the words, but also his voice still had its wonderful resonance. And, perhaps most amazing of all, is that in 2007 he sang songs in exactly the same key as he had sung them in 1980. As author and neuroscientist Dr.

Oliver Sachs said: "Music brings back the feeling of life when nothing else can." And so, in singing once more, Jerome again 'epitomized joy', uniquely experienced through songs.

Although several other songs were recorded that same afternoon, 'On the Wings of a Snow White Dove' gave both Jerome and Rosie an opportunity to share with each other, as well as the company, the profound place of faith in their lives.

> When trouble surrounds us when evils come
> The body grows weak and the spirit grows numb
> When these things beset us He does not forget us
> He sends down his love on the wings of a dove.
>
> On the wings of a snow white dove
> He sends His pure sweet love
> A sign from above
> On the wings of a dove.

POSTSCRIPT

In June 2012, when Jerome's brother Joe accompanied me on 'just one more visit', Rosie was even frailer than Jerome, who sat close to her bedside. Surrounded by the care of family, it was a time of waiting, quietly, patiently and knowingly. The joy of 'just one more song' had gone, yet in the silence, there was an unspoken sense of all they shared.

On July 12, Rosie closed her eyes for the last time, peacefully waiting for Jerome.

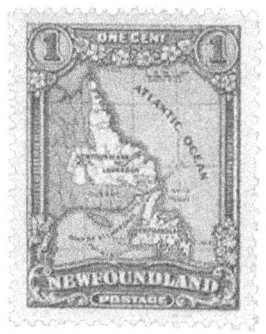

REFERENCES

Atlantic Guardian. "Atlantic Guardian visits the twin towns of Channel and Port aux Basques". *Atlantic Guardian, The Magazine of Newfoundland*, Vol. VI, No. 2, Feb. 1949, (Montreal, Quebec), pp. 39–40.

Ashton, John. "'Badger Drive': Song, Historicity and Occupational Stereotyping". *Western Folklore*, Vol. 53, No. 3, Jul., 1994, pp. 211–228.

Baker, Melvin. 'Prominent Figures from our Recent Past: James Baird'. *Newfoundland Quarterly*, vol. LXXXVIII, no. 4, (Summer 1994). Online: http://www.ucs.mun.ca/~melbaker/baird/baird.html

Behan, Dominic. *Ireland Sings: An Anthology of Modern and Ancient Irish Songs and Ballads*. London: Essex Music, 1973.

Bennett Margaret "'A Song for Every Cow She Milked...' Sharing the Work and Sharing the Voices among the Gaels" in *Sharing the Voices: The Phenomenon of Singing VI: Proceedings of the International Symposium*, St. John's, Newfoundland, Canada, July 1-July 8, 2007, Tamara Reynish, (ed), St. John's: Festival 500, 2010.

Bennett, Margaret. 'Cèilidh', definition in *The New Grove Dictionary of Music and Musicians*, London, 2000.

Bennett, Margaret. 'Living Tradition', in *Scottish Traditional Literatures*, Vol. 2, Eds. Suzanne Gilbert and Sarah Dunnigan, Edinburgh: Edinburgh University Press, forthcoming 2012.

Bennett, Margaret. 'Scottish Gaelic, English, and French: Some Aspects of the Macaronic Traditions of the Codroy Valley, Newfoundland' in *Regional Languages Studies... Newfoundland,* St. John's, Newfoundland, May l972, pp. 25–30.

Bennett, Margaret. 'So Many Steamers Ago: Memories of an English Nurse in Newfoundland in the 1930s' in *Essays in Lore and Language:* A Festschrift for John Widdowson, ed. Malcolm Jones, The Centre for English Cultural Tradition, Sheffield, 2003, pp 22–42.

Bennett, Margaret. 'Traditions of the Ceilidh', in *Celtic Heritage*, Halifax, NS, Canada, 1999.

Bennett, Margaret. *Dileab Ailean: The Legacy of Allan MacArthur*, Ochtertyre, Scotland: Grace Note Publications, 2010.

Bennett, Margaret. *Oatmeal and the Catechism: Scottish Gaelic Settlers in Quebec*, (2nd edition), Edinburgh: Birlinn, 2004.

Bennett, Margaret. T*he Last Stronghold: Scottish Gaelic Traditions of Newfoundland,* Breakwater Books, St. John's, Newfoundland and Canongate Publishers, Edinburgh, l989.

Brown, Cassie. *Death on the Ice; the Great Newfoundland Sealing Disaster of 1914*,Toronto: Doubleday, 1972. Reprinted Toronto: Doubleday, 1999.

Bruford, Alan. Review of Ian Grimble's 'The World of Rob Donn' in *Tocher*, No. 35, p. 351. Edinburgh: The School of Scottish Studies, The University of Edinburgh.

Buchanan, John Lane. *Travels in the Western Hebrides: from 1782–1790,* London: Robinson & Debrett 1793, reprinted Isle of Skye: Maclean Press, illustrated edition,1997.

Carpenter, Carole Henderson. 'Forty Years Later: Maud Karpeles in Newfoundland', in *Folklore Studies in Honour of Herbert Halpert: a Festschrift*. St. John's, Newfoundland: Memorial University of Newfoundland, 1980, pp. 111–124.

Casey, George J., Neil V. Rosenberg and Wilfred W. Wareham. 'Repertoire Categorization and Performer-Audience Relationships: Some Newfoundland Folksong Examples', in *Ethnomusicology,* (University of Illinois Press), Vol. 16, No. 3, Canadian Issue (Sep., 1972), pp. 397–403.

Child, Francis James. *The English and Scottish Popular Ballads*, 5 Volumes, Boston and New York: Houghton, Mifflin and company, 1904. Reprinted New York: Dover Publications, 2003.

Cowan, Edward J. ed., *The People's Past: Scottish Folk, Scottish History,* Edinburgh: Polygon, 1980; reprinted 1993.

Doyle, Gerald S. collector. *Old-Time Songs And Poetry Of Newfoundland: Songs Of The People From The Days Of Our Forefathers,* St. John's, Third edition, 1955.

Dundes, Alan. *Interpreting Folklore*, Bloomington: Indiana University Press, 1980.

Family Herald & Weekly Star (Montreal) 'Old Favourites', 4 July 1934, 6 August 1941 and 25 May 1949.

Ferguson, Archibald (& others) eds. *A' Choisir-chiuil: The St. Columba Collection of Gaelic Songs*, Paisley: J. and R. Parlane, 1890.

Fowke, Edith. *Lumbering Songs from the Northern Woods*, Publication of the AFS, vol. 55, Austin and London: The University of Texas Press, 1970.

Gatherer, Nigel. *Songs and Ballads of Dundee,* Edinburgh,: John Donald Publishers Ltd, 1985.

Glassie, Henry Edward D. Ives, and John Szwed. *Folksongs and Their Makers*, Bowling Green, Ohio: Bowling Green University Popular Press, 1971.

Goldstein, Kenneth S. 'On the Application of the Concepts of Active and Inactive Traditions to the Study of Repertory' in *The Journal of American Folklore,* Vol. 84, No. 331, Toward New Perspectives in Folklore (Jan.–Mar., 1971), pp. 62–67.

Goldstein, Kenneth S. *Guide to Fieldworkers in Folklore,* Hatboro, Pennsylvania: Published for the American Folklore Society by Folklore Associates, 1964.

Greenleaf, Elisabeth Bristol and Grace Yarrow Mansfield. *Ballads and Sea Songs of Newfoundland,* Cambridge: Harvard University Press,1933. Reprinted by Hatboro, Pennsylvania: Published by Folklore Associates, 1968.

Greig-Duncan Folk Song Collection, edited by Patrick Shuldham-Shaw, Emily B. Lyle & others, 8 vols., Edinburgh & Aberdeen: Mercat Press, 1981–2002.

Greig, Gavin . *Folk-song in Buchan and folk-song of the North-east,* Foreword by Kenneth S. Goldstein and Arthur Argo, Hatboro, Pennsylvania, Folklore Associates, 1963.

Greig, Gavin. *Folk-Song of the North-East: Articles Contributed to the 'Buchan Observer'*. Peterhead: P. Scogie, 1909-14.

Greig, Gavin. *Last Leaves of Traditional Ballads and Ballad Airs*. Collector Gavin Greig; edited, with an introductory essay, collations, and notes, by Alexander Keith. Aberdeen: University of Aberdeen, 1925.

Greig, John (ed. & arranger). *Scots Minstrelsie: A National Monument of Scottish Song,* 6 volumes, Edinburgh: T.C. and E.C. Jack, 1893.

Halpert Herbert and George M. Story, eds. *Christmas Mummering in Newfoundland,* Toronto: University of Toronto Press, 1969.

Halpert, Herbert and John D. A. Widdowson, *Folktales of Newfoundland: The Resilience of the Oral Tradition. 2 Vols.* St John's, Newfoundland: Breakwater, 1996.

Halpert, Herbert. 'Preface' in Michael Taft, *A Regional Discography of Newfoundland and Labrador, 1904–1972.* St. John's: Memorial University Folklore and Language Archive, 1975, pp. i–iv.

Halpert, Herbert. 'Vitality of Tradition and Local Songs', *Journal of the International Folk Music Council,* Vol. 3, Cambridge, England, 1951, pp. 35–40.

Halpert, Herbert. *Folklore: An Emerging Discipline: Selected Essays of Herbert Halpert,* edited by Martin Lovelace, Paul Smith and J.D.A. Widdowson, St. John's, Newfoundland: Memorial University of Newfoundland, Folklore and Language Publication, 2002.

Henderson, H. 'The Ballad, the Folk and the Oral Tradition' in Edward J. Cowan (ed). *The People's Past: Scottish Folk, Scottish History*. Edinburgh: Polygon, 1980; reprinted 1993, pp. 65–101.

Henry, Sam (collector). *Songs of the People*. Edited, transcribed, annotated by Gale Huntington, revised with additions and indexes by Lani Herrmann, Athens, Georgia: University of Georgia Press, 1990.

Ives, Edward D. *Joe Scott: The Woodsman Songmaker*, Champaign: University of Illinois Press, 1978.

Ives, Edward D. *Larry Gorman, The Man Who Made the Songs*, Bloomington: Indiana University Press, 1964. Reprint. New York: Arno Press, 1977.

Karpeles, Maud. *Folksongs from Newfoundland*, Hamden, Conn.: Archon Books, 1970.

Laws, G. Malcolm. *American Balladry from the British Broadsides*, Philadelphia: American Folklore Society, 1957.

Lehr, Genevieve (ed. and Collector) & Anita Best (collector). *Come and I Will Sing You: A Newfoundland Songbook*. Toronto: University of Toronto Press, 1985.

Lomax, Alan. 'Saga of a Folksong Hunter: A Twenty-year Odyssey with Cylinder, Disc and Tape'. *HiFi/Stereo Review*, Vol. 4, no. 5, May, 1960. Online: http://www.culturalequity.org/alanlomax/ce_alanlomax_saga.php

MacColl, Ewan and Peggy Seeger. *Till Doomsday in the Afternoon: Folklore of a Family of Scots Travellers, the Stewarts of Blairgowrie, Till Doomsday in the Afternoon*.Manchester: Manchester University Press, 1986.

MacEdward Leach. *Folk Ballads and Songs of the Lower Labrador Coast*, Anthropological Series No. 68. Ottawa: National Museum of Canada, 1965.

MacIntyre, Duncan. See MacLeod A., 1952.

MacKenzie, John. *Sàr-Obair nam Bàrd Gaelach: The Beauties of Gaelic Poetry and Lives of the Highland Bards* Halifax, Nova Scotia: Norman MacDonald, l863.

MacKinnon, Richard. *Vernacular Architecture in the Codroy Valley*. Ottawa: Canadian Museum of Civilization, 2002.

Maclean, Calum. 'Aonghus agus Donnchadh', *Gairm*, air. 10 (An Geamhradh, 1954), pp. 170–74 (translation, Bill Innes).

MacLellan, Angus and John Lorne Campbell (collector, editor and translator). *Stories from South Uist*. Routledge & Kegan Paul, 1961. Second edition by Edinburgh: Birlinn, 1997; reprinted 2001; 2011.

MacLeod, Angus (ed), *Orain Dhonnchaidh Bhàin: The Songs of Duncan Ban Macintyre*. Edinburgh: Scottish Academic Press for the Scottish Gaelic Texts Society, 1952.

MacNicol, the Rev. Donald. *Remarks on Dr Samuel Johnson's Journey to the Hebrides, in which are Contained Observations on the Antiquities, Language, Genius, and Manners of the Highlanders of Scotland,* London: T. Cadell, 1779.

Martin, Martin. *A Description of the Western Isles of Scotland circa 1695*. Edinburgh, 1716, Glasgow, 1884; Stirling: E. Mackay, 1934; Edinburgh: Birlinn, 1994.

McConnell, Cathal. See O'Connor, G.

McGraw, Ted. 'The McNulty Family' in *Journal of the Society for American Music*, Vol 4, (2010), pp.451–473.

Mckean, Thomas A. 'Tradition and Modernity: Gaelic Bards in the Twentieth Century' in *The Edinburgh History of Scottish Literature*, Ian Brown (ed.), Edinburgh: University Press, 2006, 130–141.

McMahon, Sean (ed). *A Little Bit of Heaven: An Irish-American Anthology*, Dublin: Mercier Press, 1999.

Meade, Don. 'The Life and Times of "Muldoon, the Solid Man"' in *New York Irish History*, Vol. 11, 1997. Online http://blarneystar.com/Muldoon6.4.11.pdf.

Mercer, Paul. *Newfoundland Songs and Ballads in Print, 1842–1974: A title and first-line Index*, MUN Folklore and Language Publication and Bibliographical and Special Series, Number 6, 1979.

Morris, Edward. '"Wings of a Dove" Writer, Bob Ferguson, Dies at 73 in Mississippi', July 23, 2001, Online: http://www.cmt.com/

Narvaez, Peter. 'Joseph R. Smallwood, The Barrelman: The Broadcaster as Folklorist' in *Canadian Folklore Canadien*, 5:1–2 (1983), pp. 60–78.

Narvaez, Peter 'Newfoundland Vernacular Song'. In *Popular Music: Style and Identity*, editors: Will Straw, S. Johnson, R. Sullivan, and P. Freedlander. Centre for Research on Canadian Cultural Industries and Institutions, Montreal, 1995, pp. 215–219.

Narvaez, Peter. 'Sony's Dream: Popularity and Regional Vernacular Anthems' in *Sony's Dream: Newfoundland Folklore and Popular Culture*. St. John's, Newfoundland: Memorial University of Newfoundland, Folklore and Language Publication, 2012, pp. 154–171.

Narvaez, Peter. "'She's Gone Boys': Vernacular Song Responses to the Atlantic Fisheries Crisis" in *Canadian Journal for Traditional Music* (1997). Online: http://cjtm.icaap.org/content/25/v25art1.html

O'Connor, Gerry and Sile Boylan (eds). *I Have Travelled This Country: Song of Cathal McConnell* (with DVD). Ravendale, Ireland: Lughnasa Music, 2011.

O'Lochlainn, Colm. *Irish Street Ballads*. Dublin: Three Candles, 1939; reprinted New York: Corinth Books, 1960; Macmillan; New edition edition 1978.

Ord, John with With a foreword by R. S. Rait. *Bothy Songs And Ballads Of Aberdeen, Banff And Moray, Angus And the Mearns*, Paisley: A. Gardner, 1930, reprinted, Edinburgh: John Donald, 1995.

Oring, Elliot. 'Review: Folksongs and their Makers', *Folklore Forum*, 1972, 5(4), pp. 156-158.

Peacock, Kenneth. *Songs of the Newfoundland Outports*, Anthropological Series No. 65, Ottawa: National Museum of Canada, 1965.

Peters, Harry B. F*olk Songs Out of Wisconsin: An Illustrated Compendium of Words and Music*, Madison: Wisconsin Historical Society, 1977.

Petrie, George and Charles Villiers Stanford, eds. *The Complete Collection of Irish Music*, 3 vols. London: Boosey & Co, 1902–5.

Pike, Robert E. *Tall Trees, Tough Men*, New York: W.W. Norton & Co., 1999.

Pike, Robert E. 'Log Drive on the Connecticut' in T*he Atlantic Monthly*, Volume 212, No. 1, July 1963, pp. 29–34.

Roud, Steve. Roud Folk Song Index. See, http://library.efdss.org/cgi-bin/textpage.cgi?file=aboutRoud

Ryan, Shannon and Larry Small, *Haulin' Rope & Gaff: Songs and Poetry in the History of the Newfoundland Seal Fishery*. St. John's, Newfoundland: Breakwater Books, 1978.

Ryan, Shannon. *The Ice Hunters: A History of Newfoundland Sealing to 1914*, St. John's, Newfoundland: Breakwater, 1994.

Scott, John. "'I Don't Think There's Anything in the World That the Common Man Will Take a Bigger Chance [For] Than He'll Take For a Seal': Some Contributions of Oral History Toward an Understanding of the Newfoundland Disaster". In *Folklore & Oral History: Papers From the Second Annual Meeting of the Canadian Aural/Oral History Association, St. John's Newfoundland October 3–5, 1975*, edited by Neil V. Rosenberg, St. John's: Memorial University of Newfoundland (1978), pp. 81–90.

Shuldam Shaw, Pat and Emily Lyle, eds. *The Greig-Duncan Folk Song Collection*, 8 vols., Aberdeen & Edinburgh, 1981-2002.

Smallwood, Joseph R. *I Chose Canada: The Memoirs of the Honorable Joseph R. "Joey" Smallwood*, Toronto: Macmillan of Canada, 1973.

Songs Of Newfoundland, a complimentary booklet of lyrics to twenty-one songs distributed by the Bennett Brewing Co. Ltd., of St. John's, NL, with the cooperation of the *Gerald S. Doyle Song Book*, St. John's, n.d. (many editions).

Sprott, Gavin. 'Traditional Music: The Material Background' in Edward J. Cowan (ed). *The People's Past: Scottish Folk, Scottish History*. Edinburgh: Polygon, 1980, pp. 54–64.

Stewart, Elizabeth and Alison McMorland (comp & ed) *Up Yon Wide and Lonely Glen: Travellers' Songs, Stories and Tunes of the Fetterangus Stewarts*. Jackson: University of Mississippi Press, 2012.

Story, G.M., W.J. Kirwin, and J.D.A. Widdowson, eds. Dictionary of Newfoundland English, Toronto: University of Toronto Press, 1982, 2nd edition with Supplement, 1990. Online: http://www.heritage.nf.ca/dictionary/d1ction.html.

Sutherland, Dufferin. 'The Men Went to Work by the Stars and Returned by Them: The Experience of Work in the Newfoundland Woods during the 1930s' in *Newfoundland and Labrador Studies*, Vol. 07, No. 2, 1991, pp. 143-72.

Szwed, John. "Paul E. Hall: A Newfoundland Song-Maker and his Community of Song," in Henry Glassie, Edward D. Ives, and John Szwed, *Folksongs and Their Makers*, Bowling Green, Ohio: Bowling Green University Popular Press, 1971.

Taft, Michael, *A Regional Discography of Newfoundland and Labrador, 1904–1972*. St. John's, Newfoundland: Memorial University Folklore and Language Archive, 1975.

Taylor, Allan, *Song, Song-writing and the Songwriter in the English Folk Song Revival*, University of Belfast (unpublished PhD), 1993.

Vallely, Fintan. *Sing Up! Irish Comic Songs & Satires for Every Occasion*. Dublin: Dedalus Press, 2008.

Western Star, The. Cornerbrooke, Aug. 31, 1904.

Winick, Steve. 'Kenneth S. Goldstein, 1927–1995', in *Dirty Linen*, No. 62 February/March 1996.

Audio and video sources

Henderson, Hamish. sleeve-notes for, *Folksongs & Music From The Berryfields Of Blair*, collected by H. Henderson.

MacIsaac, Hector and Michael Murphy (prod). DVD, *A Man You Don't Meet Everyday: Songs from the Codroy Valley*, SeaBright Productions, Nova Scotia, 2007.

Canadian Railway Songs Collection. Included 10 songs by Jim Downey, Doyles, Newfoundland. For complete list see: http://www.railwaysongs.ca/

Index of titles and first lines

ANTI-CONFEDERATION SONG	67
As I left home one morning	100
At Erinmore in the County Galway	108
At the sign of a bell on the road to Clonmel	116
BACHELOR'S LAMENT, THE	71
BADGER DRIVE, THE	61
CAMERON MEN, THE	123
Cauld winter was howlin'	83
Charlie McFadden he wanted to waltz	90
COME ALL YE JOLLY HUNTERS	120
Come all you boys from Codroy Valley	94
Did you ever hear the story about the Thomas cat?	140
EMPLOYMENT SONG, THE	100
FIVE BOSS HIGHWAY, THE	94
GALWAY SHAWL, THE	108
George O'Quinn from Grand River	132
Gussie Gale from Millville is one of the boys	111
I AM A ROVING PEDDLER	103
I ventured to walk one fine summer's morning	59
I'm lonesome since in 'Thirty-two	67
JOHN PARK HE HAD NAR' ONE	86
LABRADOR ROSE	59
MARY KATE WHITE	111
MICKY JIM MACNEIL	143
Oh, I worked up in Scotchytown	143
ON THE WINGS OF A DOVE	127
On the wings of a snow white dove	127
On We'n'sday night, March seventeen	129
PADDY HAGERTY'S OLD LEATHER BRITCHES	116
PAT MALONE FORGOT THAT HE WAS DEAD	79

PAUL E. HALL (STORY)	**77**
ROAD TO DUNDEE, THE	**83**
SEALERS' SONG, THE	**129**
TEACHING MCFADDEN TO WALTZ	**90**
There is a house upon a hill	71
There is one class of men in our country	61
There was a wee cooper who lived in Fife	150
THERE'S A BRIDLE HANGING ON THE WALL	**89**
There's many a man in the Cameron Clan	123
Things were dull in Irish town	79
THOMAS CAT, THE	**140**
TODAY	**148**
Today, while the blossoms still cling to the vine	148
We got six dollars and a half	86
WEE COOPER O' FIFE, THE	**150**
WINNIE MACNEIL	**136**

30th Annual Codroy Valley Folk Festival

Tribute to Mr. Jerome Downey

July 27, 28, 29, 2012

Recreation Complex, Upper Ferry, Codroy Valley, Route 406

"Rain or Shine - Under the Big Tent"

2 full days of *local* entertainment – fiddles, accordions, dancers, singers, etc. Local entertainment, representing folk, country, traditional and Newfoundland style music, begins on Saturday at 2:00 pm and on Sunday at 1:00 pm

Friday Night Dance
Featuring: The Islanders with Codroy Valley's own Lisa MacArthur

Dance open to all ages, bar restricted to 19 & over

Saturday Night Dance
Featuring: The Breeze Band with our own Dion Devoe, Walter Devoe, Hockey Gale, Gordon Cormier & Randell Cormier

Saturday Night Dance open to 19 and over only

Saturday
Annual Codroy Valley Folk Festival Soccer tournament

Sunday
Children's activities, games, performance hour

Admission

Individual: $7 daily pass or $15 Weekend Pass *(includes Saturday Night Dance)*
Family: $15 Daily pass   **Children under 12 free** (accompanied by an adult)

Bar and Canteen Services on site • No on site camping available

Celebrating our heritage with music

For more information contact Patsy Brownrigg 955-2061

Friday, July 27

10:00 pm   **FESTIVAL DANCE**
Featuring **"The Islanders"** with Steve Strickland, Vince Pettipas, Trent Dolomount & Codroy Valley's own Lisa MacArthur
Dance open to all ages; bar restricted to 19 and over

	Admission Fees:	
	Individual	Family
Daily	$7.00	$15.00 (Add $1 per person over 4)
Weekend	$15.00	
Dance – Daily pass on Saturday includes dance admission Children Under 12 – Free (Accompanied by an adult).		

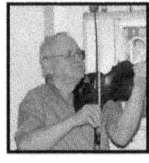

*The Codroy Valley Folk Festival and the music community of Codroy Valley suffered a great loss in 2012 with the passing of **Danny MacDonald**. Forever Remembered. Rest In Peace.*

Saturday, July 28

2:00 pm   Opening Ceremonies with Bag Pipers Sears MacArthur, Leonard MacArthur & Gordon Cormier

OPENING REMARKS

2:15 pm   CV Square Dancers with accordion player Wallace Gale
2:45 pm   The Cormier Family
3:10 pm   CV Fiddlers (Joe AuCoin, James MacIsaac, Leonard MacArthur, Wayne MacIsaac)
3:30 pm   Jr. Kendell (vocals)
3:50 pm   Ben Brake (vocals)
4:10 pm   Sears & Dwayne MacArthur
4:30 pm   Kelly Tompkins (vocals)
4:45 pm   Willie Parsons (accordion)

5:00 pm   The Bruce Family (vocals)
5:30 pm   Stephen Wall (vocals)
5:45 pm   Patsy Brownrigg (vocals)
6:00 pm   Joe AuCoin (fiddle)
6:15 pm   Leo Coffin (vocals)
6:35 pm   Mike AuCoin (vocals)
6:55 pm   Frank AuCoin (accordion)
7:10 pm   Sean & Aldonna O'Keefe (vocals)
7:30 pm   Shawna Ryan & Kenny Ryan (vocals)
7:50 pm   Jillian Chaisson (vocals)
8:05 pm   Angie Colbourne (vocals)

10:00 pm   **Dance: "The Breeze Band"**
                Hockey Gale, Dion Devoe, Gordon Cormier, Randall Cormier & Walter Devoe
           --- Dance open to age 19 and over only ---

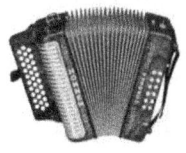

Sunday, July 29

1:00 pm	Youth Performance Hour
2:00 pm	CV Fiddlers (Joe AuCoin, James MacIsaac, Leonard MacArthur, Wayne MacIsaac)
2:20 pm	Don Crewe (vocals)
2:40 pm	Stan Pearce & Family (mandolin, fiddle, vocals)
3:00 pm	**JEROME DOWNEY TRIBUTE**
3:30 pm	Hector MacIsaac (vocals)
3:50 pm	Freida Bungay (Mandolin)
4:05 pm	Lisa MacArthur
4:25 pm	Jr. Kendell (vocals)
4:50 pm	The Mamas (vocals)

5:10 pm	Dion Devoe (vocals)
5:25 pm	Dwayne & Sears MacArthur
5:45 pm	The Bruce Family
6:10 pm	Ben Brake (vocals)
6:30 pm	Vanessa MacArthur (vocals)
6:45 pm	Kelly Tompkins (vocals)
7:00 pm	James & Wayne MacIsaac (Fiddle)
7:15 pm	Mike AuCoin (vocals)
7:35 pm	Patsy Brownrigg (vocals)
7:50 pm	Frank AuCoin (accordion)
8:05 pm	Angie Colbourne (vocals)
8:20 pm	The Cormier Family
8:45 pm	Malorie Johnson (vocals)
	AG Time (Anything Goes!!!!)

- Performers and times are subject to change
- Youth Performance Hour – Pre-Registration is required
- **The Codroy Valley Recreation Association** is hosting the 4th Annual Codroy Valley Folk Festival Strawberry Cup - Saturday, July 29 & children's games and events on Sunday, July 30 at 2:30 pm – 4:30 pm.
- Breakfast at the Oceanview Seniors Club - Sunday, July 29 - $5.00/person.
- St. Ann's Guild will be selling cold plates on the festival grounds on Sunday, July 29 - $7.00/person

For Further Information – Contact:
Patsy Brownrigg (955-2061)

COLLEGE OF THE
North Atlantic

A CD of the complete audio recording collection
can be obtained by the purchaser
of the paperback edition

Jerome Just One More Song!
Local, Social & Political History in the Repertoire of a Newfoundland-Irish Singer

by

Send or email your address and proof-of-purchase

to

GRACE NOTE PUBLICATIONS C.I.C.
Grange of Locherlour,
Ochtertyre, Crieff
Perthshire, PH7 4JS
Scotland, UK

www.gracenotepublications.co.uk
books@gracenotereading.co.uk

NOTES

www.ingramcontent.com/pod-product-compliance
Lightning Source LLC
Chambersburg PA
CBHW071227200426
R18167400002B/R181674PG43193CBX00002B/1